innovatechurch

innovatechurch

Jonathan Falwell,
General Editor

B&H
PUBLISHING GROUP
Nashville, Tennessee

978-0-8054-4826-9

Published by B&H Publishing Group,
Nashville, Tennessee

Dewey Decimal Classification: 254
Subject Heading: CHURCH ADMINISTRATION \
CHURCH GROWTH

1 2 3 4 5 6 7 8 9 10 • 12 11 10 09 08

CONTENTS

OUTREACH

CHURCH PLANTING

APOLOGETICS

CULTURE

PRAYER

An Innovation of Ideas and a New Commitment to the Foundations

by Jonathan Falwell

May 15, 2007, is a day that will be forever etched into my heart. It was a day that turned a page in my ministry life, as well as in my personal life. It was the day that my father, mentor, pastor, boss, and hero went home to be with the Lord. When I awoke that morning, I had no idea that by the end of that day my life would be thrust into a whirlwind of incredible new challenges. This was not only because I lost my dad, but because I would soon be called as the pastor of one of America's largest and most respected congregations.

To say that I was petrified at the prospects of being the senior pastor of the church where my dad had served for nearly fifty-one years would be an understatement. How could I step into that pulpit? How could I step into the shoes of a man like Jerry Falwell?

This was not a transition for which I was prepared. Not only was I reeling in pain from the sudden loss of my dad, but I had the added pressure of a new and high-profile job. I literally needed a supernatural intervention to help me. I can tell you without hesitation that the supernatural intervention I needed came in ways I could have never dreamed or imagined.

In the months following my dad's death, we began to see an outpouring of God's blessing on Thomas Road Baptist Church like none I had ever seen or experienced. Each Sunday we saw hundreds of people flooding the aisles for salvation or a renewing of their commitment to Jesus Christ. During the eight months following my father's death, we saw more than three thousand people accept Jesus Christ as their personal Savior, more than eighteen hundred people join our church, and nearly nine hundred people publicly profess their faith in Christ through baptism. Our church was listed as one of the fastest-growing churches in America—not a small feat for a church that already had more than twenty thousand members. I was stunned at what God was doing at our church!

I knew that those results had nothing to do with my abilities or talents, understanding that these blessings came directly from the hand of God moving in our midst. Through these miraculous days at Thomas Road Baptist Church, I began to search out what was happening to try to understand whether it was something that could be sustained and/or duplicated.

Was it a fluke? Or was it a heaven-sent response to a heartbreaking experience in the life of our church? I can honestly say that, during the first few months in my new role, I found myself almost embarrassed by the results we were seeing. I didn't want to even publicly discuss what God was doing at Thomas Road because it didn't seem right to me since my dad was not here to experience it. I was confused because I believed that Dad should be the one presiding over the physical and spiritual growth we were experiencing.

As you might imagine, I spent a great deal of time trying to process why this great outpouring was underway. Through those days, I began to seek out Scriptures that could help me understand what God was up to in our small town of Lynchburg, Virginia. It was then that I came across a verse in 2 Corinthians that summed up what God was doing among our church: "Not that we are competent in ourselves to consider anything as coming from ourselves, but our competence is from God" (3:5). That is the clearest representation of the work of God in a church, or in someone's life, that you can find. It is not anything we can do; it all comes from Him.

My dad led our church for nearly fifty-one years based on the truth that it was never about Jerry Falwell—it was always about Jesus Christ. And so, my timidity to share what God was doing began disappearing and I started to shout the story of the movement of God within our congregation every chance I got. I began to understand that this was not a story about Jonathan Falwell or Thomas Road Baptist Church; it was rather a story about our great God who can do great things even in the midst of great tribulation.

In fact, I believe that what is happening at Thomas Road Baptist Church today can be tracked all the way back to the earliest days of the church. In 1956 my dad founded this small-town church with just thirty-five adults. He then went out and knocked on every door in Lynchburg to tell people about the new church and what Jesus Christ had done in his life and the lives of the church's members. Because of his audacious faith and the willingness of the congregation to follow their intrepid young pastor, God uniquely blessed that small congregation. I became fascinated in the processes and programs that dad used to stimulate growth and nurture believers, especially since it was now my responsibility to continue with the vision that started on the warm summer day years ago.

In reviewing the church's history, it is clear that neither Dad nor our congregation ever shied away from innovation. When

Dad said God had called him to launch a Bible college, the congregation was on board with the plan. The church was prepared to confront the culture, as well, by establishing a home for unwed mothers, a Bible-based dwelling for alcoholic and drug-addicted men, a K-12 Christian school, a cutting-edge broadcasting center, worldwide evangelistic programs, and others.

Last fall I participated in a panel discussion at the National Outreach Convention in San Diego, California. This panel, put together by Ed Stetzer, was aimed at discussing what it meant to be an innovative church. On the panel were several pastors and associates who were serving in large churches that were having a real impact in their communities. While the discussions were varied that evening, everyone on that panel agreed that innovative ministry should never chip away at the purpose for the church, which is the spreading of the gospel. The "good news" of Christ is the hope of the world for the individual and for the country. Our country needs a radical transformation and the only way to radically change the country is to radically change the values of the people that make up the country. The gospel of Christ is what is needed.

The Pew Forum on Religion and Public Life recently released a study that examined the state of churchgoing in America. Of the thirty-five thousand adults questioned, 16 percent claimed no religious association, while a quarter of those in the eighteen- to twenty-nine-year-old age range said they do not belong to any organized religion. Compare these numbers to a similar survey by the National Opinion Research Center in the 1980s, in which only five to eight percent of Americans were unassociated with a religious faith, and you see that America is rapidly becoming a secular nation. The Pew Forum noted that of the 16 percent not claiming a religious association, half actually *turned* from the religion in which they were raised. The study concluded that "the United States is on the verge of becoming a minority Protestant country."

The Pew report also found that men are "significantly more likely than women to claim no religious affiliation," with nearly one-in-five men claiming no formal religious affiliation, compared with roughly 13 percent of women. Further, younger Americans are turning their backs on religion. Among those saying they are unaffiliated with a particular religion, 31 percent were younger than age thirty, and 71 percent were age fifty or younger.

It is evident that people in our nation are looking outside our churches for answers. I believe this is largely because of the effort to bring about "tolerance" and "diversity" in the hearts and minds of Americans. The problem with this, in terms of faith, is that when we accept all teachings as equal, the message of the gospel is greatly weakened. People don't need churches when they are on their own personal "spiritual quest" for enlightenment. The problem with this viewpoint is obvious because Jesus did not claim to be "a way" to heaven. He claimed to be "the way" to heaven (see John 14:6). We must take this message to every person.

As I write, talk show queen Oprah Winfrey is promoting a book titled *A New Earth*, which is being called a publishing sensation. About 3.5 million copies of the book, written by Eckhart Tolle, have been shipped, largely because of Winfrey's promotion of it. Brian Tart, president and publisher of Dutton Publishing, which published the book, told the Associated Press that Tolle and Winfrey were scheduled to lead Internet seminars that were to begin on March 3, 2008. "Oprah herself has committed ten weeks to talking to the author, and people from all over the world will be able to participate," said Tart, who added that more than half a million worldwide had registered for the seminar. Tolle says he is not aligned with any particular religion or tradition. His influences, he says, include mystical Islam, Sufism, Zen Buddhism, the sayings of Jesus, and other writings.

It is apparent that the truth of the gospel is not welcome in our politically correct society that embraces all "truth" as equal. If ever there was a time when Christians—real Christians—need to be looking to innovate their evangelistic efforts, it is now. We must uncover new ways to share the Good News of Jesus Christ in our churches, our homes, and our society.

In today's church world, I fear that there are growing numbers of pastors who are stepping outside the boundaries of the core values of the church, just for the sake of being innovative. Some are leaving behind the intrinsic truths that are foundational for a local body of believers. Innovation should never shun the foundational truths of the faith, including:

1. the inspiration and inerrancy of the Scriptures (The Bible was written by men divinely inspired and is God's revelation of Himself to man without error.)
2. the virgin birth and deity of Christ (Jesus was born without a sin nature and was fully God and fully man.)
3. the substitutionary atonement of Christ (When Jesus died on the cross, He was dying for the sins of the whole world—past, present, and future.)
4. the bodily resurrection of Christ (Jesus was seen by more than five hundred people after His resurrection, proving that He was God.)
5. and, last but not least, the imminent return of Christ (Christ could return at any moment to set up His kingdom and, when He returns, He will judge the whole world in righteousness.)

These truths make up the building blocks of doctrine that form our core beliefs. To hold these beliefs and not to talk about them is like seeing a man drowning in the ocean and not throwing him a life preserver. Beliefs determine behavior. If we believe these truths "delivered to the saints once for all" (see Jude 3), we must then be about the business of acting on the beliefs. We can be innovative in our methods and our approaches of conveying these truths, but we cannot innovate (change) the message. I would like to propose that being innovative means being true to the message and being creative in the presentation of the message. In fact, God is a creative God.

When we are passionate about God and His message, He will give us creative and innovative ways to connect with the world, at large. I would also propose that we are not being innovative when we change the message. That is not being innovative, that is being influenced. *Innovate* means to "introduce something new."[1] When a church is sharing the life-changing message of the gospel of Christ, the result will be lives that are being innovated by the power of the gospel. The gospel has the power to change a person's perspective from hopelessness to hopefulness; from anxiety to peace; from conflict to resolution; from having no purpose to being full of purpose. Jesus said, "I have come that they may have life and have it in abundance" (John 10:10).

Some churches have narrowed their vision. They are focusing only on maintaining their flock. As a result, they are not influencing many areas of their communities with the gospel. We cannot lead our churches under a mantle of fear or trepidation about how our message may be received. We must look to the apostle Paul as our mentor in boldly taking the gospel to all areas of society.

Our goals of innovation should come through methods of invigorating our worship experience or finding new means to plant churches or discovering new manners in which we can confront the culture through "salt and light" ministry. My passion is to use the innovational methods described in this book to help pastors and church leaders around the nation to consider new means of taking the gospel to their own communities.

During my journey of discovery regarding the fifty-one years of innovative ministry at Thomas Road Baptist Church, I found that the church has always been active within eight major areas of ministry. I believe these eight areas, as defined in this book, should be the backbone of every church's desire to become more proactive in outreach and Christian influence.

In my humble opinion, churches can reach their greatest potential and purpose by fully engaging in all of these areas. We cannot afford to cherry-pick the areas of greater interest. Further, we must be involved and passionate about all of them, especially those that require us to step outside our comfort zones. I think many churches need to relearn the basics so that they can reinvigorate their efforts to impact their communities with the gospel.

In this book we will attempt to make the case for all eight of these areas. It is my deep desire to cast the vision to pastors and laypeople everywhere to get involved in all of them to fully experience your church's potential for Christ. I trust that you will study this book, meditate on its points, thoughtfully process its premise, and ultimately begin to implement its designs and methods.

While the title of this book talks about innovation in the church, the real innovation comes from taking our churches back to the future. Found within our roots are foundational truths that will guide our churches to greater heights in the days to come. While I am fully supportive and engaged in using brand new methods to reach the lost in our nation and world, I am also fully aware that those methods can never trump what is not new—the basics that have worked for ages. Innovating (or altering) the foundational message of the gospel is simply not an option.

Notes

1. http://dictionary.reference.com/browse/innovate.

LEADERSHIP

CHAPTER 1

Overcoming Discouragement in Order to Lead

by Jonathan Falwell

In 1998 Gary L. McIntosh and Robert L. Edmondson wrote a book titled *It Only Hurts on Monday: Why Pastors Quit and What You Can Do about It.* The authors found that the demands and difficulties of ministry were so great that many pastors were unable to properly cope with the challenge. The title of the book came about when one pastor, who was asked how his ministry was going, replied, "It only hurts on Monday."

I'm sure most pastors understand that sentiment. Sundays can be difficult days for many pastors. And men who are unprepared to function in the multifaceted and trying world of a pastor typically do not remain in the ministry. Mondays become days of recovery and healing for many battered pastors. It would be easy to get discouraged if one's ministry was weighing this way on someone.

A few years ago pollster George Barna found that the average lifespan of a pastor in 1993 was only about four years. They just weren't prepared for leadership. In their book McIntosh and Edmondson found that loneliness, burnout, an inadequate education and unrealistic ministry expectations were among the key reasons former pastors cited for giving up the ministry.

Writing as a man who has, on occasion, wondered whether I was really prepared to lead a church—and a church that my father lead so graciously and naturally for more than half a century, at that—my heart goes out to men who have found themselves so burdened by ministry that they were unable to carry on. I'm sure there are many pastors in our nation today who are discouraged in ministry or even on the brink of quitting. I want to direct this portion of our book on church innovation to them.

I believe the primary reason behind the discouraging rise of pastors either defaulting or stepping down from their roles is that they did not receive the proper training to prepare them for the treacherous job of leading a flock of believers. It certainly is not a job for those without proper grounding—and thick skins.

Tragically there are many *former* pastors in our nation who bear deep scars gained in ministry. I believe many of these battle scars can be avoided if pastors are properly and prayerfully prepared for leadership. In this chapter I want to focus on four key commitments to which every pastor needs to adhere so that he is equipped to lead his congregation. I want to examine what I call four "Non-negotiable Commitments" that I believe pastors need to make to themselves and to God.

Non-negotiable Commitment 1: "I will remain spiritually intimate with my Savior."

A senior pastor is mandated to provide spiritual guidance and instruction to his congregation (see 2 Tim. 4:2). At the same time, a senior pastor is supposed to personally live out what he preaches so the people within his congregation can have a concrete example to follow (see Phil. 3:17). Therefore, I believe that it is difficult (and probably impossible) for a senior pastor to encourage his people to cultivate a spiritual intimacy with the Lord if he is not spending time in intimate worship with Jesus Christ.

A pastor cannot get so involved in the good and honorable work of the ministry to the point that his efforts replace the necessary one-on-one time with God. Too many pastors have neglected their personal growth in Christ in order to facilitate the spiritual growth of their flock. This leads to spiritual stagnancy. And when a pastor gets to such a point, he will soon discover that his leadership becomes ineffective. As pastors, we must determine that we will make time for our own focused time with Christ.

When I think of this commitment to remain spiritually intimate with my Savior, I often find myself reflecting on our Lord's words to Martha in Luke 10:38–42:

> While they were traveling, He entered a village, and a woman named Martha welcomed Him into her home. She had a sister named Mary, who also sat at the Lord's feet and was listening to what He said. But Martha was distracted by her many tasks, and she came up and asked, "Lord, don't You care that my sister has left me to serve alone? So tell her to give me a hand."
>
> The Lord answered her, "Martha, Martha, you are worried and upset about many things, but one thing is necessary. Mary has made the right choice, and it will not be taken away from her."

Martha was doing an honorable task of preparing dinner for the Lord. And there was certainly nothing wrong with her desire to make ready a meal for Him. Even so, our Lord gave His own assessment of the weight of each task. Jesus provided an evaluation of working rigorously versus growing spiritually.

Jesus emphasized that cultivating intimacy with God should always be the priority in our lives. First, Jesus taught Martha, "But one thing is necessary." He made it abundantly clear that saturating your mind with God's Word is not simply a *nice* thing to do; it is a *necessary* thing to do.

Second, Jesus taught us, through His conversation with Martha, that saturating our minds with God's Word is not simply a *good* choice to make; it is the *best* choice to make ("Mary has made the right choice").

Third, Jesus showed us that saturating our mind with God's Word will not simply make a *temporary* impact; it will make an *eternal* impact ("it will not be taken away from her").

I believe that Jesus' words in this passage are crying out to pastors, especially those who are in need of encouragement. He is calling you to spiritually support your service to Him! Pastors, we must lead from a heart that remains intimate with our Savior. That intimacy comes only from regular *quantity* time with Him.

Non-negotiable Commitment 2:
"I will always preach against sin, even when it becomes unpopular."

As a ministry grows, senior pastors are sometimes confronted with the temptation to water down the truth of the gospel, either for the sake of popularity or conformity. That is why a pastor must hold this commitment close to his heart and remind himself of it every time he stands up to preach the Word of God. My father often said, "God didn't call me to be popular; He called me to be faithful."

Within the first year after I became shepherd of the Thomas Road Baptist Church flock, this non-negotiable commitment began to resonate in my heart. In fact, I was so passionate about standing upon biblical doctrine that I intentionally scheduled a sermon series that would serve to bolster my commitment to preaching the Word to a generation that has come to believe that truth is often relative. This series was titled, "iTruths: Life Lessons for the iPod Generation."

I based this sermon series on three verses that I believe should be imbedded into every pastor's mind:

- John 8:32: "You will know the truth, and the truth will set you free."
- John 14:6: "I am the way, the truth, and the life. No one comes to the Father except through Me."
- John 6:68–69: "Lord, who will we go to? You have the words of eternal life. We have come to believe and know that You are the Holy One of God!"

The pressure to compromise on biblical truth can come from unlikely sources and at improbable times. And so a pastor must be committed to standing on the truth of God's Word.

Non-negotiable Commitment 3: "I will not minister to my church at the expense of my family."

This is a very practical but vital commitment that must be made prior to entering the ministry, especially the senior pastorate. I frequently tell my congregation that I will always hold to the belief that the order of priorities for me as a pastor is this:

God first.

My family second.

My ministry third.

Isn't it interesting that when God lists the qualifications of a pastor in 1 Timothy 3, there is more elaboration surrounding the qualifications related to the pastor's family than any other qualifications? I believe God wants us to make sure we give solemn thought to our families' spiritual growth. It is always heartbreaking to learn of a pastor with a prominent ministry who has failed to properly lead his family.

Not long ago I was asked to travel along on a Christian cruise where I would speak to a number of other pastors. I saw this as a great opportunity for Christian fellowship and to take my wife and children on a vacation where we could spend some quality time together. One morning, prior to one of my speaking times, I made sure that my wife, Shari, and our four kids were where they needed to be on the ship. I then made my way to the ballroom where I was to speak. Just before I was to step to the podium, though, I noticed my youngest son, Nicholas, standing at one of the ballroom doors. I slipped out to see what was wrong. He was upset because he couldn't find Shari, who was apparently not where I told him she would be. I asked a friend to walk Nicholas down to that area to help him find his mother and everything seemed OK.

I returned into the ballroom and was introduced to speak. However, just after I began my presentation to the pastors, someone approached me and whispered that Nicholas was back in the hallway, crying uncontrollably. I apologized to the audience and quickly walked off the stage. My son was still upset and he wanted me. Let me tell you, that group of pastors was important to me, but not nearly as important as my son. I spent the rest of the afternoon with him because I felt it was the most important thing I could do that day.

This is the mind-set that we must all have as pastors. We must protect our families at all times. We must be there for them when they need us. My dad asked a very important question from the pulpit on several occasions: "What would it profit a pastor to gain the whole world and lose his own children?" This simple paraphrase of Scripture is one that I hold dear. A pastor must always ensure that his wife and children have an emotional and spiritual foundation that they know will never fail.

Non-negotiable Commitment 4: "I will not quit when I feel defeated."

Building a ministry takes time, patience, endurance, and prayer. It is hard work and, at times, can be physically, emotionally, and spiritually grueling. In fact, I doubt that a person who has never served as a pastor can fully understand the burdens that we sometimes bear. Here's the good news: God is bigger than any of the problems we face in ministry.

My dad was a faithful leader, one that never compromised on truth but never failed to reach out in compassion to those who had fallen. It is my prayerful intention to also serve at Thomas Road Baptist Church for as many years as the Lord gives me breath and ability (unless, of course, He calls me to another duty). Pastors cannot base their ministry lives on the cut-and-run mentality that is so prevalent in our society. A pastor must be committed to his flock, without thought of personal gain or future reward. Pastors must be willing to stay the course for as long as God calls them to service in their place of ministry.

Of course, pastors are going to face challenges—and some huge ones, at that. The Bible tells us that "man is full of troubles." Pastors aren't immune to the struggles of life. In fact, our troubles are more acute because we must not only deal with the problems we face, but also those that many in our congregations face. And so we must be ready to allow God to see us through our storms, instead of leaving our post when the challenges become severe and trying.

Pastors need to make a personal contract that says: "Quitting is never an option." This contract means that we will not walk away in the face of adversity. It means that we will stand firm on God's Word, confident that it is He whom we serve.

I want to address a couple of questions that may arise in the minds of pastors reading this book.

Question: What if I have already compromised in these commitments?

Answer: Confess your shortcomings to God and commit to change, with His help, today. We worship the God of the second chance, third chance, fourth chance, and so on. Just look at the life of Peter or Paul or Matthew or King David to see how God was willing to forgive and bless. He doesn't want to cut you down and leave you bleeding in the dirt. God not only forgives and restores, He empowers those who desire to serve Him with wisdom and understanding to make the right decisions in the future. This is how we gain godly wisdom. Don't let past failures or doubts weigh you down. Cast your burdens on Christ and carry on in ministry.

Question: I have made these types of commitments to my ministry. But how can I ensure that I remain true to them?

Answer: Rehearse these commitments regularly and renew them daily so as to tether your heart to them. As the writer of Hebrews says: "We must therefore pay even more attention to what we have heard, so that we will not drift away" (Heb. 2:1).

It is a humbling thought to realize that, as leaders, virtually all things in our lives and ministries rise and fall on our ability to lead. For several years prior to my father's passing, I served on the Thomas Road Baptist Church staff in a variety of positions. As I served alongside him, I felt a certain freedom because I always knew there was someone above me who would use great wisdom in making the important decisions for our church. I knew that he never made a crucial decision apart from prayer.

Now that I am in the same role as my father, I realize with new clarity the heady truth that leadership is sometimes not very fun. The fact is that I am not capable of leading this church and making the important decisions for our congregation apart from constantly leaning upon Christ.

In 2 Corinthians 3:5 (NKJV), we are told, "Not that we are sufficient of ourselves to think of anything as being from ourselves, but our sufficiency is from God."

Pastor, has ministry worn you down? Are you struggling to find or rediscover your footing in ministry? Do you feel like you are unable to properly lead your congregation? If so, please allow me to remind you that you are not sufficient to come out of your distress alone. Apart from casting your cares on our great God and allowing Him to minister to you and lead you through whatever trials are afflicting your ministry, you will almost surely fail.

But there's hope! I encourage you to reclaim 2 Corinthians 3:5 and remember that your sufficiency is indeed from God. In my brief tenure as senior pastor at Thomas Road Baptist Church I have needed to be reminded of this great truth on many occasions. Whenever I am facing problems in ministry, I take time to focus on this wonderful verse. As a result, my greatest joy is knowing that God is working through me. Allow Him to have His way in your life. Humbly recommit to serving Him and I assure you that you will discover amazing new joys and blessings in ministry.

CHAPTER 2

Leading from the Middle of the Pack

by Dr. Doug Randlett

I graduated from college back in the 60s. After a year of graduate school I ended up at a small Christian college in Fresno, California. My first position was that of a classroom instructor and the school registrar. I clearly remember dealing with people that were doing business with the school. A person would ask me how old I was. Here I was at a mere twenty-two, looking more like a fifteen-year-old kid, overseeing a part of the school administration. This was my inauguration into the world of "middle of the pack" leadership.

After a stint at a Bible college in Tennessee, I accepted my first full-time church ministry position in 1970. I have been in continuous church ministry since that time. My positions have varied: Minister of Music, Associate Pastor, Youth Pastor, Church Administration, Director of Ministries, Campus Pastor of a megachurch multisite, and presently an Executive Pastor. Over these nearly thirty-eight years of continual Christian service, each of these roles has provided great experience at this thing we call "leading from the middle of the pack."

Those of us who serve from the middle of the pack are not senior pastors. God has called us to be subordinates to our leaders, just as Jesus drew unto Himself twelve men whose roles were to help Him in ministry. And within this area of service, there are many truths that we must understand.

My favorite writings on this subject are in a book by Dr. John Maxwell titled *The 360-Degree Leader*. I was amazed at how he so thoroughly hit key issue after key issue that I had experienced in my years serving as a church associate. I can remember thinking, "I wish I had written this book." It was through the reading of that book that I decided to put on paper some important lessons I have learned as one of these "middle of the pack" leaders.

As a foundation to those lessons, it is important that something is said about the relationship of managing and leading. Throughout most of my career, I was told that I was a good manager. Reading leadership books, I once had the opinion that I could be a leader or a manager, but not both. This misconception played nicely into my personal insecurity. I had determined that my "lid" was in management and that I could never serve as a leader. It took years of experience, with much coaching and teaching, to help me see that the two concepts are not mutually exclusive. It is indeed possible to lead and manage.

I was teaching a class for new members and noticed a gentleman highly engaged in what I was teaching. As it turned out, he was a retired businessman from a successful securities business. We struck up a friendship, and in the process he offered to mentor me in my leadership skills. Over the next three years, Larry Stephens helped me to see the difference between managing and leading. He coached me in taking my innate management skills and tweaking them to accommodate the need for me to lead. Today, in my role as the Executive Pastor of Thomas Road Baptist Church, I owe much to those mentoring years that served to prepare me to lead from the middle of the pack.

I want to examine some principles I have learned through my various roles.

Principle #1: Attach your wagon to the right horse.

In teaching for nearly twenty years at Liberty University, I have had numerous students that did not understand this principle. In fact, I have had pastors and associates consult with me about accepting a call to a particular church where they fully, if unintentionally, planned on ignoring this principle.

What I mean by attaching your wagon to the right horse is this: you need to minister in a church that not only has the same ministry philosophy (like "Purpose-Driven," for example), but also does ministry that is compatible with your style of ministry. Too many associates choose a ministry because they have an invalid messiah complex. They essentially say: "I'll solve their problems and I'll straighten them out." Rarely does this work.

One lesson to learn comes from the old saying about reading the wind. If the wind is blowing north to south, it will probably never change to blow east to west by your presence or your efforts. No matter how good your motives are or how hard you try, the wind will continue to blow north to south. As I was once told, "It is what it is." The principle of the wind applies to senior leadership in a church. It is what it is. Therefore it is your responsibility to find a ministry "blowing" the same direction you want to go or else know that you must accept the different direction.

A real estate motto fits this principle: Location, location, location. The best value of the real estate is probably the one with the most desirable location. To my readers, I wish to say that there is a church ministry opportunity that offers the best ministry value to you because it has the greatest potential for the ministry gifts you bring to it. It is much like a golfer and his glove. He gets one with the highest quality that fits his hand perfectly. In the same way, you should look for a "hand in glove" ministry.

Those of us who are not senior pastors are not in the best seat to affect the culture and ministry style of the church. Therefore it behooves us to find a church that is heading in the ministry direction that God has called us to pursue and sign on with that body of believers. God uses many different church models to accomplish His goals. But there is one more suited to each of our gifts and preferences.

When you are mismatched with the church where you serve, the only outcome is ultimately negative. They will look for a convenient way to move you out, either by highlighting your weaknesses or releasing you because you speak poorly about the leadership of the church. Neither of these options edifies you or the church. To position yourself for success as a leader in the middle, you need to be in a ministry position that will best facilitate that success.

Principle #2: Your vision must reflect the vision of the senior pastor.

This sounds reasonable enough, but it is a barrier to success for many "middle of the pack" leaders. We all have our own vision for what we want to accomplish for the kingdom of God. Too often we desire a ministry situation where the senior pastor has a hands-off policy. This way you can spend your energy and time on your own agenda. However, if your senior leader has a hands-off approach, it is possible that he is not a visionary leader who can move the ministry forward.

Your role is to discover your leader's goals, make them your goals, and make your leader a success by helping him to accomplish them. Many years ago Gordon Luff was the youth ministry director for Thomas Road Baptist Church and Liberty University. This is the first principle I remember learning from him. He would say something like this, "As a youth pastor it is my job to discover the goals of Jerry Falwell, make them my goals, and make him a success as I accomplish them."

I saw that, as an associate, my vision must fit within the context of the greater vision cast by the senior leader. You are not a lone ranger or a free agent. Your success as a leader is tied to fulfilling the vision of the senior leader.

You ask, "Does my vision matter at all?" Of course it does. But once again let me remind you how important it is to minister in the right location. Here at Thomas Road Baptist Church I work with Pastor Jonathan Falwell. Before I took this position, it was my responsibility to discover his vision and goals. Once I understood how closely they resembled my own vision and goals, the decision to come here was an easy one. When my goals reflect my leader's goals, then in reality I am expending energy each day in fulfilling my vision, as well.

Principle #3: Leadership approach—Relational.

As church ministry associates, we understand that our primary role involves people. This includes both those in direct ministries and those in support ministries. Relationships are at the heart of what we do. As associates, we are the working interface between our senior leader and the staff.

A dear friend of mine drove this lesson home. Joe Ryan retired early from business and became the business administrator at my church. He was brilliant in understanding the nuances of church business. Yet, at heart, he was a minister.

I remember the day he gave a profound illustration. He held up a pencil and told us that no matter how busy we were (the pencil represented all our work needing to be done), if someone walked through our office door, we were to place the pencil down and give our undivided attention to that person. The work will be there when the conversation is over, he said. He reminded our entire staff that we are in the people business.

People are more important than programs. Our ministry emphasis should weigh on the side of people rather than procedures, policies, or programs. If this is true in reference with our church constituents, it is equally true when leading our staff.

I have found over the past forty years that the most effective leadership tool is leading through building relationships. When the relationship is established, you have positioned yourself to face any challenge or opportunity with that person. For me, both "yes" and "no" responses are better received when delivered by someone I trust. This principle does not dictate that each staff member be considered your best friend. What it does infer is that you understand each other at a level that facilitates candor and open communications.

Relational leadership for an associate minister can often be more effective than hierarchical leadership, possibly because by definition the associate does not sit at the top of the hierarchy. I believe in the power of the person over the power of position in leading. Your staff will not be impressed with your title unless they have confidence in you as a person. My leadership is a direct expression of my relationship with the staff. Recently I spent some time with a staff member to teach or remind him that the greatest asset of this ministry is our staff. We often say that our greatest asset is our congregation. I believe, as associates, we must build into our staff or else we weaken the chain at its most important link, because it is the staff that interfaces with our congregation.

I recently told my assistant to protect me from interruptions so I could do some writing. I said to interrupt me only for an emergency. In the last hour of that day, one staff member came in, apologetically, but needed an answer to a sticky situation. I laid down my "pencil" and helped him with his problem. An hour later, I took a break and met with a counselee that called. The situation was one that needed immediate attention. So once again I laid down the "pencil" and made people a priority over my writing project.

As an illustration of building staff relationships, I was spending time with a staff member working on a ministry agenda. It came time for lunch, at which time I invited him to have lunch with me.

During that time we put aside the agenda, spending time getting to know each other better. It is my goal as a leader to get to know each staff member beyond our professional interaction. My wife, Jane, and I have a goal to spend social time with each staff couple for the sake of building our relationship at the personal level.

My senior pastor is a very busy man. But I have noticed that in the midst of his hectic life, he has established an open-door policy. If any one is justified to have a closed-door policy, it is Jonathan Falwell; but he understands and embraces the importance of relational leadership. We must find a way to help our staff understand that they are more important than the program.

Principle #4: Celebrate the power of team.

Megachurches are often described as personality driven and therefore may have a senior pastor that is viewed as an autocratic leader. It may be better stated that they are not autocratic as much as they are exhibiting what is called "founder's syndrome." If your senior pastor is a founder whose personality defines the congregation, this role lays strictly with him. However, as associates, we cannot lay claim to that position; consequently, there is no case to be made for autocratic leadership in the middle of the pack.

Team leadership is far more effective than autocratic leadership when leading from the middle of the pack. We usually have a significant number of staff and volunteers that we lead. For success in ministry we do well when we get our team members to develop a personal sense of ownership for their portion of the ministry. This often happens when the leader places emphasis upon the importance of the team.

Developing a team is no easy task. I remember a number of years ago when a colleague of mine noted that we were all on the same team. I rarely saw this individual on a day-to-day basis and had little knowledge of his specific role within the ministry. Apparently what he meant by the word *team* was that we were all located on the same piece of property. It had nothing whatsoever to do with us functioning in concert.

The developing of a team can be likened to basic training for the military. The purpose of this training is to help each staff member see the importance of working together, supporting one another, and cheering each other along in accomplishing the goals of the church. The ancient Greek army can shed some light on this concept of understanding the power of team. In the New Testament, the Greek word *paraclete* is translated "comforter." We refer to the Holy Spirit being our Comforter. But in ancient Greece this same word was used differently. The Greek army would reference a soldier in battle needing a *paraclete*, which referred to another soldier fighting at his back making certain he was never attacked from his unprotected side. In the same way, we in ministry need to function as a "paraclete" to other staff members, making certain we cover their backs.

When a team has developed this power, there will be a spirit of unity, team chemistry, and a collective force that helps us to accomplish more than we would as individual staff members or individual departments. The "middle of the pack" leader is responsible to facilitate such an environment.

How do you go about creating such an environment? It begins with your vision for the staff and extends to your guidelines and hiring practices. You need to hire people who want to work together. In addition to hiring people of godly character and job competency, it is necessary to evaluate them from the perspective of team chemistry. Chemistry is too often underestimated or totally overlooked in its importance to ministry success.

Team chemistry is often confused with hiring people we want to be with—people we enjoy. The priority is the chemistry and not my personal choice to work with a friend.

Recently I was consulting with a pastor friend that had developed a relationship with a potential staff member. The qualifications of this person did not fit any priority need in the ministry of that church. To take funds earmarked elsewhere would have negatively impacted the morale of the team. As nice as it might have been to have a "buddy" on staff, to do so would have hindered the potential effectiveness of the team. That pastor made the right decision not to hire that person and is presently positioned to build a strong team.

Obviously hiring involves matching people to the needs of the ministry, based upon their gifts and abilities. To build a strong team, the associate must be continually aware of his personal strengths and weaknesses and add to the team those who will complement and build up in the areas needed. Some leaders have a tendency to hire below their own talent level. That is, 10's tend to hire 9's, 9's hire 8's, 8's hire 7's, etc., until the quality of staff is eroded because of personal insecurity. The wise associate will look to hire staff equally or more talented than themselves.

Jim Collins, in his book *Good to Great*, talks about getting the right people in the right seats on the "bus." To develop this powerful team, you may need to move some people to different seats on your ministry bus. Some staff members may be less than effective team members because they have simply been placed according to need and not according to giftedness and ministry fit.

When I took the position of Executive Pastor at Thomas Road Baptist Church, I began the process to get several staff members into the right seats on the bus. I am constantly evaluating each team member's passion and ministry giftedness. This process will often result in moving a staff member to a different position and/or to a different accountability structure. If you are fortunate enough to have made a good evaluation, you will receive affirmation from those staff members that have been affected. They will be more fulfilled in their roles, and the net result will be that they buy into the team concept because they feel like key contributors to the goals of the team.

Experience shows the value of having regularly scheduled staff meetings with your team. These meetings do not have to be lengthy nor chock-full of information or teaching. The purpose of these meetings is simply to have a consistent touch point for your team. As they share victories in their ministries and prayer requests for personal and ministry needs, a sense of spiritual togetherness develops that no other activity can match. I cannot overstate the role these times play in helping the staff to be sensitive to their common frailties. We are all in the same boat and need each other for support. These meetings do not produce overnight results. It is the collective result of meeting regularly that brings about a team attitude.

Principle #5: Lead staff through "shared leadership" instead of "team leadership."

While I just discussed the power of team, it may seem a contradiction to now talk about shared leadership over team leadership. I suggest that there is a nuance of difference between these two that is worth pointing out.

Please understand that in shared leadership, as the leader of the team, I do not relinquish my responsibility or authority. As the saying goes, "The buck stops here." In fact, I can still bring my proposed agenda to the table. But instead of my dictating the agenda, the team is given an opportunity to speak to that agenda. It may come in the form of clarification, amplification, additions, or subtractions to the proposed agenda. The idea is that the team takes ownership of the agenda, thereby increasing the probability of successful implementation of the agenda.

My experience as both a leader of a team and a participant is that leaders often have a desire to sell their agenda to the team. There was a generation that responded to that style of leading. It is my opinion that today's young leader wants a greater voice in the process. This is why I call this process "shared leadership." With this approach, two important things are communicated about them as individuals. First, they are valuable team members; and secondly, that the leader also values their input. This affirmation is important and perhaps even critical for staff retention and for the implementation of the team goals.

At the end of the day, you, the leader of the team, will be expected to make the final call on decisions. The team can speak to the agenda, but you will carry the responsibility of pulling the trigger. Knowing this causes me to value the team's advice and input. I find that the better data I have, the better decisions I make.

Principle #6: Subordinate leaders must communicate effectively.

It is the responsibility of each staff member to communicate and share ideas, suggestions, criticisms, and concerns to the appropriate person. Having served nearly forty years in a subordinate position, this was a lesson I learned early in my career. It would be wonderful to think that our senior leader has nothing better to do than to check up on us and ask how he can make life easier for us. Well, that is just not the nature of being a senior leader.

An associate pastor I knew was disgruntled over his financial situation, believing he was not getting appropriate salary increases. It was suggested to him that he go to his senior leader and make his case. He responded with, "My pastor knows where my office is. If he wants me, then he can come to my office." To my knowledge, that situation was never addressed or rectified. This is a classic illustration of someone missing this principle.

As a young associate pastor, I understood that my leader had on his shoulders the entire responsibility for the church. He had more than a full plate. The last thing he needed was the added expectation that I might think that he was going to track me down to see how my life was going.

Part of my success as a subordinate leader is my ability to consistently communicate issues that should be addressed, as well as good reports from the members of my team. It is my job to have wisdom and a sense of timing in what I communicate and how often I communicate with my leader.

One of the joys of being the senior leader is to get positive news from the various church departments. It is my role to have current data from each ministry and strategically present updates to my pastor. He does not need to hear every detail of what is happening in the church. He will want to have numerical growth data, key stories of spiritual victories in the church, and anything worthy of celebrating with the entire church.

As for sharing problems and challenges with the pastor, I give you a warning: be careful. You need to learn what he needs to know and on what issues you need his advice. You need to learn the best vehicle in communicating church issues. It may be through e-mail, voice mail, or an in-person discussion. It is up to you to study your leader and make wise determinations in this regard. Your pastor does not need to be bothered by every ministry "hang-nail." Be certain that any issue you bring to attention is "senior pastor worthy." There is an art to this, and it will take time for you to master this point.

Timing is a major factor. A given issue may be important to share, but the time to discuss it needs to be considered. Some agenda items may sit on your list for several days or weeks. When to present them can take on spiritual aspects. Often times I simply have a spiritual sense that today is not a good day to present a particular item.

Dr. Elmer Towns taught me the principle of "three hearings." Sometimes the first hearing gets no response. The second hearing may bring a "yes," but you are not certain that the yes is final. At the third hearing it could go in either direction. The best response to the third hearing is: "I already approved that." I've used this principle religiously on major issues and have found it to be a valuable tool in quality communication with my leader.

Principle #7: Loyalty is not based upon ignorance.

As associates, we may be prone to see our leader as "having it all together." We may think they are brighter, faster, and more effective than we. Therefore, if we discover that they have personal weaknesses and leadership failings, we become alarmed. We need to face the reality that no one is perfect and that we all have personal and leadership weaknesses.

This principle teaches that loyalty to a leader is not based upon your ignorance or denial of those weaknesses. A good leader is comfortable knowing that staff members have some knowledge of his weaknesses. That comfort comes from teaching your staff that loyalty to the leader and knowing the leader's weaknesses are not mutually exclusive thoughts. You can be fully aware of his weaknesses and choose to be loyal.

Once I understood that it was okay for me to know that my leader was not perfect, it freed me to choose a lifestyle of loyalty toward my leader. I have always understood human frailties from a scriptural perspective, but to understand it from a subordinate's perspective was something I'd given little thought to until my friend, Dr. David Adams, taught me this many years ago.

Loyalty based upon appropriate knowledge of the weaknesses in my authority has caused me to be more prayerful for him and more protective of his reputation. I do not entertain gossip about his weaknesses. I choose to be loyal, making every effort to magnify his strengths and fill voids in his leadership.

Principle #8: Be a problem solver for your team.

My role is to knock barriers out of the way for my team so they can more effectively and efficiently fulfill their goals. These barriers may be financial, structural, programmatic, or relational. It is my responsibility to feel the pulse of every ministry under my care. I need to be aware at all times of what is going well, what is not going well, and what needs to be changed or adjusted. Regular interaction with your team members is necessary.

I have used a simple agenda approach with team members to help me eliminate barriers. I ask questions such as: "What went well in your ministry this week?" "What did not go well in your ministry this week?" "Do you have a plan to solve what did not go well?" "Are there other priorities that need addressed?" "What can I do to assist you in solving ministry problems?"

That last question opens the door for my team to share barriers to success. I look for what I call "low hanging fruit." That is, could I quickly solve something for them to enhance their ministry experience?

In a recent meeting with a key staff member, I asked what I could do to help that person be more effective in ministry. Their response was how they needed upgrades in their media equipment in order to minister more effectively to the students. It was not a huge request either in amount of equipment or amount of money needed to solve the problem. Within a short time, I was able to facilitate the addition of the needed media equipment. It was "low hanging fruit" but was a valuable addition to effective ministry. In the director's mind, a huge barrier had been removed.

Principle #9: Never stop growing. Have a mentor and be a mentor.

This principle reminds me again of two dear friends to whom I have referred earlier in this chapter: Larry Stephens and Dr. David Adams. These two men have uniquely ministered to me as mentors.

Larry Stephens is my most recent mentor. This retired Christian businessman saw leadership potential in me that few others saw. He offered himself as a mentor. As good as that offer was, it was not the key to my success as a leader. The key was my willingness to place myself under his direction as an instrument of growth and to make critical adjustments in my leadership. I had to have a willing spirit to grow as a person and as a minister.

Pride is the greatest enemy of growth. As a "middle of the pack" leader, we are subject to developing a sense of pride in our chosen field of expertise. When taken to the extreme, that sense of pride will prevent us from seeing our need to have someone in our lives to assist us in growing to the next level.

Ideally, you will choose to have a formal mentor in your life. The mentor may be someone that is simply older than you and has more life experience. A mentor can also be someone that has greater expertise than you. Or that mentor may be someone who has greater wisdom and can advise you on decision-making issues. The mentor is not there to make you an expert at leading, but to help you see your potential and to open your eyes to your reality.

In life's journey, you may notice that you have informal mentors, as well. In my life I can name several. First, there was Dwight Riggs, my roommate during my freshman year who taught me about my call to ministry and how to define a love relationship. Next came Chester Phillips, pastor during my first ministry position, who taught me to "take a little mud with the rain." That is, do not think life will always be rosy. There was also Jerry Falwell, one of the busiest men I have ever known, who taught me never to let ministry rob me of being a godly family man. I think of Dr. Tom Mullins, Senior Pastor at Christ Fellowship, where I served nine years. He taught me that the most important thing I can do for people is to add value to their lives. I could name others, but I ask you, "Can you name some mentors in your life?"

Dr. David Adams, my leader for sixteen years, taught me another mentoring principle. He would say, "Randlett, wherever you go, take someone with you." What he meant by that was that, as a leader, I should always be mentoring someone else along the path of growth. I was Dave's young Timothy, his mentoree. By his gesture, he was telling me that I had value to kingdom causes. Each of you should be helping a younger, less experienced leader in the paths of growth that you have already experienced.

There is a principle akin to this that teaches leaders that one of their primary jobs is to work themselves out of a job. If you are insecure as a person in a leadership role, you will not agree with this philosophy. But mature leaders understand that a leader is defined in part by his ability to raise up other leaders. Mentoring is the road to raising up next-generation leaders. If, indeed, you work yourself out of a job, do you not know that God already has the next step of your journey waiting for you?

The Reward

Leading from the middle of the pack is extremely rewarding when you fully understand the principles of servant-leadership. As a subordinate leader, you have the opportunity and responsibility to practice biblical servant-leadership each day. As you do this faithfully, you will experience the joy of seeing your team do great things for God, and you will receive a "well-done" from both your earthly leader and your heavenly Leader.

CHAPTER 3

Everything Rises and Falls on Leadership

by Jonathan Falwell

As pastors, we must be attuned to the spiritual direction of those with whom we minister at our churches. We must ensure that our staff members are as committed as we are to the four "Non-negotiable Commitments" I detailed in chapter one. We must also work to ensure that our leadership staff is fulfilled in their callings and working in tandem with us.

Let's examine some key ways in which pastors may make certain that their staff members are focused on ministry.

The goal in helping our staff to succeed and grow is similar to the goals for our personal growth. We want to see our staff grow personally in their spiritual lives, grow professionally as ministers, and grow in their ability to develop and equip the lay staff. Your priority in developing staff will be with those that most closely interact with you. If your church staff is growing, they will be involved in nurturing the growth of other staff and the members of your church.

As the senior leader of the staff, we set the pace for leadership development by providing a living example as we grow in the Lord. Do not underestimate the power of being a model for leadership development. The members of our staff watch us more closely than we often realize. So our personal plan to grow as leaders is probably being observed at all times by our staff.

To foster growth and respect with my ministry team, I place an emphasis on including them in the process of strategizing and fulfilling our ministry goals. As they see me including them in key discussions and critical ministry decisions, they feel a part of all that we are doing and understand my dependence on them. When they realize how much I depend on them, this fosters their spiritual focus.

The senior pastor should have a consistent approach to leadership development. It is my experience that the Thomas Road staff is more supportive of my leadership when I am consistent in my leadership style.

I mentioned that staff development must be done intentionally. It does not happen by wishful thinking. We, as senior leaders, need to give time to this area. There is no such thing as a staff development "magic bullet." There are a variety of ways to ensure that your staff is growing and committed to the same ministry goals:

- Read a Christian-themed leadership book together;
- Discuss the topics of the book together;
- Attend leadership seminars or conferences;
- Conduct focused staff meetings;
- Pray together and share your burdens;
- Regularly encourage each other.

You may wish to pick a unique area upon which to focus ministry growth over the course of one year. As an example, if your church is disconnected from the church goals, you may want to study churches that have a simple and effective model of achieving church goals. Or if your church is experiencing a time of numerical growth, you may want to develop staff effectiveness at recruiting and placing new lay leaders.

At Thomas Road Baptist Church, we are experiencing a time of amazing growth. Many younger families are joining our church on a weekly basis. As our church is entering its fifty-second year and has many long-running practices aimed at members who have been with us for years, we do not want to stop anything that is working for these members. We also do not want our "old ways" to become a type of lid for continued growth. And so our staff is growing and developing in the ability to look at new ways to do ministry to accommodate our growth spurt. We must continue to develop and learn in this area. This is an exciting time for our staff as their leadership cultivates efforts to meet our new challenges.

I often use time with staff members, in both formal and informal settings, to look for teachable moments for leadership development. When a staff member shares a ministry situation that needs to be addressed, I may use that occasion to give the member some coaching on how to deal with the issue. Applying wisdom during these encounters will help you to assess a potential environment for growing staff. This type of "coaching" is equally successful when done with an individual staff member or with a group of staff members.

An area often neglected in regard to the leadership development of staff members is the area of budgeting. Once again, as the senior leader, we are called upon to direct the church in the stewardship of finances. We are responsible for seeing that funds are sufficient for operational expenses, mortgage payments, salaries, missions, evangelistic outreaches, and departmental needs. In the attempt to be simultaneously generous and frugal, it is easy to neglect the need to budget for staff development.

We should view staff development as a worthy investment. The potential to grow our church is linked to the growth of our staff members. The benefit of a growing staff may be seen in a number of ways. If staff development is budgeted sufficiently, the payoffs will more than make up for the financial commitment.

Thomas Road Baptist Church regularly invests in developing staff members as we finance them to periodically attend conferences and seminars. These opportunities are aimed at improving a specific area of leadership development, either a personal growth need or something to improve ministry.

We also provide time away for several staff members to use their gifts and abilities to minister at other churches. These times away help the staff members hone skills that otherwise may not be developed in service at our church. Not only is the church where they minister being blessed, *we* are blessed by their further knowledge when they return. They come back refreshed, affirmed in their giftedness and often bring back new and innovative ideas from the other ministry.

Finally, it is my observation that clear and effective communication by the senior pastor with the staff is critical to their growth. Jesus plainly spoke with His disciples. And while they may not have fully understood all that He was saying at the time, they were prepared to carry about His will after His resurrection and departure to heaven. When communication is ineffective in our families, they suffer. Likewise, when communication is ineffective with our staff members, they suffer in their ability to minister. As senior leaders, we must communicate our love for our team, our affirmation of their accomplishments, and our support for their effort. When we accomplish this, we will see positive staff development that carries into every area of our churches.

Developing Your Lay Leaders

As pastor, I am humbled by the privilege of leading this church my father planted. As earlier noted, I admit to sometimes being a bit nervous in this role. I'm not uneasy in the sense that I don't believe in the power and provision of God. Rather, I sometimes get a little anxious that I might do something to mess up what God is doing. I imagine many pastors have had similar thoughts. We don't want our personal weaknesses to ever get in the way of what God is doing. This reaffirms our need—my need—to ensure that we are always casting our cares on Christ. As I stated, we will surely fail if we attempt to lead our churches apart from total dependence on Christ.

With this heavenly reliance in mind, I have seen the importance of having godly leaders around me and developing godly lay leaders throughout the entire church. My dad, who was also discerning in placing godly men in his midst, regularly stated, "Everything rises or falls on leadership."

As pastors, we must be prayerfully developing the team that God has given us. In order to ensure that we don't miss out on what God wants to do in the lives of the people in our churches, pastors may want to consider this Action Statement that carries three action verbs: "Win. Grow. Send." As the senior leader, it is a key role of the pastor to keep his entire church focused on accomplishing these directives.

Win

Winning people to Christ drives everything we do as a ministry. If people aren't being won to Christ, we may as well close the doors to the church. Evangelism is the starting point for church and for every person. Romans 3:23 tells us that "all have sinned and fall short of the glory of God." Every person has a sin nature and, without accepting Christ, we are destined to be separated from God for eternity. But the "good news" of the gospel is that Christ, through His death and resurrection, paved the way to eternal life for all who will believe. Our first job as a church and as a ministry is to proclaim His message to everyone in our communities.

Our church pioneered a concept we call "saturation evangelism." This means we are to take "every available opportunity to win every available person to Christ using every available means."

We have also been one of the pioneering ministries in the use of radio, television, education, direct mail, and the Internet in proclaiming the message of Christ. We use a combination of "go and tell" ministries and "come and see" approaches to share the message of Christ. Further, we have training classes that intentionally develop the members of our church to become leaders in sharing the gospel with people they know. We have dozens of teams that go out every week to share this message and we have more than one hundred and fifty weekly community outreach groups that are sharing the love and message of Christ.

Dr. Elmer Towns developed a term called "FRAN-gelism." We utilize this concept at our church by encouraging our members to invite their Friends, Relatives, Associates, and Neighbors to join us. Thom Rainer, in his book *The Unchurched Next Door*, says that eight out of ten people would come to church if they were invited by a friend.[1] Our church recently sponsored a "Friend Day," in which we saw thirty-two hundred "friends" visit our services. That means that thousands of our members took the initiative to invite someone they care about to join them at church. We are passionate in our commitment to win people to Christ.

Grow

Evangelism will almost certainly lead to numerical growth, but numerical growth is not the primary mandate of the church. According to the Great Commission, we are charged to "make disciples" (Matt. 28:19). In this passage we are told to go, baptize, and teach the disciples "to observe" everything that Jesus taught. We most fully develop as a Christian when we can see good examples up close and personal.

One of the biggest challenges in a megachurch is to grow larger and smaller at the same time. By this I mean that a growing Christian needs times of corporate church worship as well as times of personal attention that is served in smaller groups within the church. If a church has thousands of adults, it might need hundreds of groups that focus on the individual needs of people. Presently at Thomas Road Baptist Church, we have hundreds of groups where men, women, boys, and girls can connect relationally with one another.

All of these groups require adult leaders who have been trained in discipleship development. We are constantly recruiting and training new leaders. This, of course, is not unique to large churches. Even the smallest churches need to be working to develop leaders who can serve in specific roles, enhancing the ministry of the pastor.

In the past few months, we have started more than thirty "adult Bible communities," with plans to add twenty more within the next six months. Each of these new medium-sized groups contains within it smaller groups of people who meet together with the focus of challenging each other to grow spiritually on a personal level.

"Everything rises and falls on leadership." To cultivate a healthy church, you must develop healthy leaders who develop healthy members.

Send

The directive to "send" is the culmination of winning people to Christ and helping them grow in their faith. The natural progression of growing in Christ is to become passionately committed not only to the *person* of Christ, but to the *mission* of Christ.

Thomas Road Baptist Church has sent thousands of believers to the mission field and we have trained thousands of pastors to go into existing churches. Additionally, in partnership with Liberty University and Liberty Baptist Theological Seminary, we have planted hundreds of churches in the last three decades.

In fact, we have made a new commitment to church planting just within the last few months.

Have you ever heard of a BHAG (pronounced *B-Hag*)? My dad loved to reference this term. It is an acronym for the phrase:

Big

Hairy

Audacious

Goals

Since my dad's passing, we have developed our own BHAG: to plant five hundred churches over the course of the next five years. This "sending" effort will take a huge amount of prayer, focus, and energy. But by God's grace, we are committed to carrying out what we feel is God's call on our church. I am passionate about winning people to Christ, helping them to grow in their faith, and sending them out to participate in the mission of Christ. Our staff, our lay leaders, and our congregation are equally as passionate about this design for ministry. Working in one accord, we desire to infiltrate our nation with new Bible-believing churches.

Notes

1. Thom S. Rainer, *The Unchurched Next Door* (Grand Rapids, MI: Zondervan, 2008).

CHAPTER 4

Leading the Volunteer Family

by Matt Willmington

Picture this.

Let's say I've just gotten married, and my wife and I sit down to plan out our life together. At the top of the list is the type of house we have always dreamed about. We both want a large house, with several rooms, a spacious kitchen and family room, and a sprawling lawn.

One thing becomes clear—owning this house will demand a lot of cleaning, upkeep, and maintenance. We both have developing careers, so our time is limited. We could hire people to help, but we don't want to spend our money that way.

We hit on the perfect solution—we'll have children. Sure, they'll require more of our attention as infants, but soon they'll be able to cover the cleaning chores. We think three should fill the order.

Years go by, our plan has worked perfectly. Then we begin to dream again. We really could use a backyard pool, with patio and

English garden. Of course, the three children already have their hands full with chores, so . . . you guessed it—we decide to have more children to cover the new work.

Ridiculous? It's true that in past generations families in agricultural societies have sought more children to help run the farm. But is that the fundamental reason to have children? To handle the household chores? We'd be judged pretty shallow, if not abusive, parents if that was our family planning strategy.

But isn't that the way many church leaders view their volunteers?

Before we talk about enlisting, equipping, and engaging workers in your church, you must address this fundamental question: What is my "volunteer-vision"?

How do you view the volunteers in your church? What is their mission? Why do you want more of them?

I'll share my concern with you. Too often I have witnessed leaders viewing volunteers as merely cogs in their programming machine, worker bees to build their . . . I mean, GOD'S kingdom! They are like the parents in the story—they want children, but only for the labor benefits.

So let me test you:

Volunteer-vision question #1

Do you see volunteers as providing slave labor or as family members performing chores? In fact, mark your position on this spectrum (put an *x* on the line). Be honest, how do you see, how do you treat volunteers?:

_____

slave labor   *family members*

Slave Labor or Family Chores

What difference does it make? How you view volunteers will determine how you lead them.

If I see my volunteers as servants, then their mission is to do a job. They exist to build my church. They are slot-fillers, a numbered person assigned to a task. To enlist them I use a strong sales pitch, or a pinch of guilt. To keep them engaged in serving, I use verses about "putting your hand to the plow and not looking back," and "taking up your cross and following." Quitting is not an option. We need to burnout for God. After all, it's all for the ministry.

But there is another view.

I could see my volunteers as children of God, members of the family. Jesus called His disciples "friends" (John 15:15). Yes, servants of God, but not *my* servants. In this view, people volunteer out of devotion, not duty. Serving is not an assignment; it's a part of the family chores. It's not an activity I choose if I want to be more spiritual, or out of guilt. Rather, it's part of the everyday life of a growing Christ-follower. Serving is a course in my spiritual growth, and I perform it out of love for the family, for my neighbor, and for my Master.

I would argue that if you shift to this second vision, you and your volunteers will greatly benefit. You'll have more peace and focus as you recruit, train, and place your people, because you will be thinking more of their growth than your task list. Your people will serve out of joy because they'll feel your true love and concern for their growth. Balance will replace burnout in their lives.

You will actually be leading, shepherding your people in the way that Scripture teaches, and in the way Jesus modeled.

I heard a prominent pastor frame the choice this way:

> "You can use your people to build a great church, or
> you can use your church to build a great people."

The choice is yours. But you know my advice. Innovate your vision of volunteers. View them as their Master does.

And once you do, we can move on to some of the nuts and bolts of leading volunteers. With our new volunteer-vision we can *connect* and *coach* them.

Connecting Volunteers

Organized volunteerism is on the decline in America. According to the Bureau of Labor Statistics of the U.S. Department of Labor, the percentage of Americans who serve through an organization has declined over the last five years, to a low of about 26 percent of the population (roughly 60 million people). And that number includes anyone who reported that they volunteered at least *once* in the past year. So the actual number of people who volunteer regularly, or weekly, is much less.

About 29 percent of women volunteered in the past year, compared to about 22 percent of men. For more comparisons, look at the groups most likely and least likely to volunteer:

People most likely to volunteer:

- women
- people ages thirty-five to fifty-four
- married people
- parents with children under eighteen
- college graduates
- people with part-time employment

People least likely to volunteer:

- men
- people in their early twenties
- never marrieds
- people with no children
- people with no high school diploma
- unemployed

(Source: Bureau of Labor Statistics of the U.S. Department of Labor, http://www.bls.gov/news.release/volun.nr0.htm.)

The good news is that the main organization type for which people volunteered was religious/church in nature. The less heartening news is that people volunteered an average of one hour per week of their time.

We have our job cut out for us in the area of connecting our people into serving commitments. So what are the best methods for tackling this?

We've seen our need to view and treat volunteers as family rather than slaves. But there is another question for you:

Volunteer-vision question #2

Do you have a culture of serving or a checklist for serving? Have you created a whole atmosphere in your church where volunteerism permeates, and everyone knows about his or her serving responsibility? Or do you merely have a checklist of jobs, and people do not hear about serving until you have the pressing need to "fill a slot"? Mark your position on this spectrum (put an x on the line):

I have a culture of serving   I have a checklist for serving

A checklist approach to serving is usually driven by the slave-view of volunteers. It's fueled by the programs church leaders continually throw on their people, and the desperation of leaders to cover the jobs. Volunteers in these churches suffer from burnout, but another problem is short-term commitments. If I am always filling the recruiting list for emergency ministry positions, people won't settle in to long-term service.

When you have the family view of volunteers, you'll more naturally create a culture of serving in your church. People will understand the importance and benefits of serving as a normal part of the Christ-life.

Think of the difference in this way. Which church would you rather lead?

- A church where the people sit and wait for you to make an impassioned sales pitch to a service project, and where they commit to ministry only after you have designed and promoted a program to address a need. If it's not listed in the bulletin or the church calendar, they don't do it.
- A church where the people know how to serve each other and the community, and do it with little prompting from you. In an every-day fashion they visit each other in the hospital, make meals for the sick, fix the car of the single mom next door, share their faith at work, and send their money to help build wells in Africa.

I know the second church sounds a little too good to be true. But it is possible, though hard work, to have a church like the second example: read Acts 2. The church had just been birthed, and by the end of the chapter you read about the way they served each other. It continues though Acts 4 and throughout the New Testament. And because there was a culture of serving, when there were special needs, they could then be easily filled by the checklist approach.

In other words, Acts 2 was the predecessor of Acts 6.

The church was already in the cadence of serving when the need in Acts 6 arose for special ministry through the meals-for-widows program.

So how can we innovate a culture of serving? How can we connect volunteers? *Model, teach, pray, scout, invite.*

1. Model: I worked for several years at a new church plant in metro-Atlanta. For the first eight years of the church, we had no building and had services in two different public school facilities. Every chair, piece of staging, sound equipment, and nursery furniture had to be set up each Sunday morning and torn down that afternoon. To help create a culture of volunteerism, our staff modeled serving every Sunday. We helped set up and tear down right beside our army of incredible volunteers.

Jesus exhibited this "leading from the trenches" model. He ministered alongside His disciples, and then gave them the ultimate serving picture in John 13 as He washed their feet.

2. Teach: Paul, Peter, John, and the other early church leaders/authors taught often about serving. They gave instructions such as these:

> Based on the gift they have received, everyone should use it to serve others, as good managers of the varied grace of God. If anyone speaks, his speech should be like the oracles of God; if anyone serves, his service should be from the strength God provides, so that in everything God may be glorified through Jesus Christ. (1 Pet. 4:10–11)

> We have different gifts, according to the grace given us. If a man's gift is prophesying, let him use it in proportion to his faith. If it is serving, let him serve; if it is teaching, let him teach; if it is encouraging, let him encourage; if it is contributing to the needs of others, let him give generously; if it is leadership, let him govern diligently; if it is showing mercy, let him do it cheerfully. (Rom. 12:6–8 NIV)

We can teach serving during the Sunday services, in our small group studies, through brochures, volunteer information centers in our lobbies, church Web sites, etc.

How can you teach it to your people?

3. Pray: It's the most obvious, most powerful, most simple, and most neglected step in connecting volunteers. We see the need, we feel the burden. We know our people need to be drawn in to their family responsibility of serving by God's Spirit. So Who better to talk to than God Himself?

Jesus modeled this leadership step for us in Matthew 9:35–38. We are to ask God to send His children to work in the field. In Luke 6 He again modeled it as He prayed all night before selecting the twelve volunteers who would accompany Him.

How much time are you devoting to praying for volunteers?

4. Scout: As a leadership team our eyes should always be on the flock, looking at who would fit where in serving. Again, we believe that serving is a vital part of their discipleship, and we want to match people's gifting with the opportunities available.

Looking back at the Acts 6 story, the church leaders told the people to look around within the church, and identify seven men who fit the job description. Paul was scouting in Acts 16 when he heard about a dynamic young disciple from Lystra named Timothy, whom he added to his team.

Are you spending time with your leadership team scouting your people, constantly looking for ministry matchups?

5. Invite: It all comes down to this step—the "ask." People will connect when they are simply asked to. This sounds contradictory to the culture of serving, but it's not. At some point we have to invite people to take their step of obedience. The volunteerism survey from the Bureau of Labor Statistics found that the majority of volunteers stepped up to serving because someone asked them to.

Jesus practiced this very clearly and at times abruptly. The calling of each of His key students were short conversations, almost "drive-by" recruitments. "Drop your net, leave the tax booth, climb down from the tree, let's go! I have new assignments for you" (see John 1; Matt. 4).

The invitation should not be from guilt, arm-twisting, and an empty sales pitch. Surveys and probably your experience show that making worker recruitment announcements during the Sunday morning service yields the weakest results. People do respond to emergency needs or pleas from the pastor to help in children's ministry, but it ends up an impulse commitment—sincere but short-lived. Personal invitations are still the most persuasive and sincere.

Does your staff regularly, personally invite people to join them in their ministry adventure?

Coaching Volunteers

In connecting people with serving, they are giving something to me. But in coaching people in their serving, I am giving something to them.

If I spend my energy creating a culture of serving and connect people to ministry, but never train and encourage them in their jobs, I am sending the slave-vision message—"I just want you working; I don't really care about you." Not only that, but if I am unleashing an untrained army in my church and on my community, someone's going to get hurt! There will be spiritual malpractice and personal burnout because my volunteers simply do not know what they are doing.

Coaching, then, is a critical component of leadership. It moves us from leading people *into* ministry, to leading people *in* their ministry.

Let's consider three stages of coaching: basic training, ongoing training, and retraining.

1. Basic training: When a person does take the step toward serving, are you ready to coach them? It requires much more than putting the group study material in their hands and pushing them into the middle school room. The attention I give them at the beginning of their service can greatly enhance their experience and can set them on the road to healthy ministry. Here are some effective parts of this early stage:

- *Assessment*—Using applications and inventories, find out who this person is, what's their story? What gifts, abilities, experiences, and passions do they have? Where in the ministry would they experience the "sweet-spot" fit?
- *Interview*—Nothing replaces a face-to-face talk. Spend time listening, hearing the life of this person.

- *Background check*—In this day it's important to have a system of checking people's references and records. This is crucial for anyone serving around children and students. Some potential volunteers may find this slightly offensive, but most understand the benefit. Explain that we all do this for the physical safety of our children, the emotional health of our parents, and for the reputation of each volunteer.
- *Orientation*—Meet with each new volunteer, preferably in small groups so that they can begin to form teams. Clearly explain through teaching and handbooks these items:
  - An overview of your particular ministry, its history, vision, mission, values, etc.
  - The ministry programs, activities you lead
  - The list of serving jobs in your area
  - Any expectations on their commitment, such as standards, schedule, and so on
  - A clear job description of what you are asking them to do
- *Observation*—Allow the person to visit your ministry area, watch a program in action, see what it's like to sit through vocal team practice, hang out with high school guys, try their skill at parking lot duty one Sunday.
- *Trial run*—If you both are feeling good about their involvement, give them a 30-day commitment. See how they respond being immersed in your ministry. If it's a good fit, move forward. If not, move a different direction.

Let me interrupt our conversation about training at this point to throw in a related volunteer-vision question. You are in the process of assessing and assigning new workers to various ministries. Where are you placing them? Are you balanced in the way you are lining them up with serving opportunities? Which ministries are getting the most volunteers, which are getting the least? Was that on purpose or an oversight? And a bigger question:

Volunteer-vision question #3

How many volunteers are you connecting and coaching for serving *inside* the church? How many volunteers are you sending *outside*, to the community? Where are your volunteers serving? Mark your position on this spectrum (put an *x* on the line):

INSIDE—in church ministries   OUTSIDE—in community projects

What's the point? Where you have your volunteers will tell where your church's mission and priorities are. Is your church seen as an organization that exists to serve itself, or does your community see your church as a Good Samaritan who serves its neighbors?

2. Ongoing training: Now the game really gets started. Your volunteers are excited, engaged, and charging full speed ahead. So what do they need for the long haul? This is where we remind ourselves again that these people are not slaves—they are family. We care not only for their effectiveness in ministry, but also for their personal growth. We coach them in three areas:

- *Life development*—They are first and foremost disciples of Jesus. So, we "disciple" them. We encourage their growth through personal teaching. We make sure they are worshipping in, not working through every church service. We help them balance their serving time with family time. We invest in them through parenting seminars and marriage enrichment retreats. We ask them how they are doing. Over the years I have used variations of this "dashboard." It's a quick life report I've handed out in weekly meetings. It gives me a snapshot of how people are doing and what I need to address:

My DASHBOARD

Name: Date:

Rate yourself in these areas for LAST WEEK . . .
E=lousy   1/4=poor   1/2=fair   3/4=good   F=great

MY MINISTRY "TANK"

_____ Productivity
_____ Time management
_____ Fruitfulness

MY RELATIONSHIP "TANK"

_____ Spouse
_____ Kids / family
_____ Group life
_____ God (prayer/study)
Reading in Scripture now . . .

MY REST "TANK"

_____ Physical health
_____ Emotional health
_____ Sabbath quality

- *Skill training*—We continually fine-tune, upgrade, and improve their ability to minister. We use weekly meetings, seasonal training events, Web-based learning, podcasts, books, etc., to keep their skills sharpened. These include:

- Technical skill—media, small group leading, band, video, teaching, Web development, guest services, etc.
- Social skill—understanding age characteristics of my flock, group dynamics, etc.

- *Team building*—The entire volunteer endeavor is based on team—remember, it's a family? This serving team is an expression of the body of Christ, and it's on the playing field of spiritual warfare. We must constantly spend time nurturing the relationships between the family members. We use meetings, retreats, exercises, and assessments to show the team each member's value, and the way to function most cohesively and efficiently.

3. Retraining: Even in a culture of serving with the best volunteer-vision, at some point a change is needed. People need change, a break from the routine, a new mission. Too often we don't recognize this need and keep asking the same service from the same people in the same way. That's a surefire recipe for running down the volunteer's engine.

> A path becomes a rut,
> A rut becomes a sidewalk.

What was once an exciting spiritual adventure of serving, over time, becomes a well-worn, boring trip. And then we get locked into a ministry commitment that is etched in cement. As a consultant recently commented to me, "The way we treat volunteers, it's no wonder they feel like they've been 'sentenced to ministry'!"

So what do we do as leaders? Be prepared at different times to innovate your workers' experience.

- *Refresh*—Simply said, give them a break! Sabbath your volunteers. Watch for seasons in their lives where they just need a break. It's okay to rest, to take a few weeks or even months off of serving in your area. If that sounds weak to you, or makes you panic, go back to our volunteer-vision questions.

- *Retool*—A major change in your church direction, a new ministry launch, a new development in a technical field—many events can signal the need for you to pull the team off the field and spend significant time in giving them new skills.
- *Redeploy*—The time will come when God wants to send your volunteers into a new assignment within your ministry, or to a totally new and different ministry. Do you care enough to reassign them? Do you care enough to release them to God's new adventure for them?

This story paints the retraining points in my mind.

I served at Thomas Road Baptist Church for several years, then for eight years at West Ridge Church in Dallas, Georgia, and now I'm back at Thomas Road.

When we finally moved into our first building at West Ridge, it was a day of celebration. We met in school buildings for eight years, and over that time we developed an impassioned, die-hard family of volunteers, hundreds strong. We knew in moving into a new facility—the first building that was "ours"—that we didn't have to set up and pack away every week, we would have volunteer retraining challenges. And we did. Some of it we got right; some of it was more difficult. Most of the teams made the transition with focused retraining by our staff in the weeks and months leading up to the grand opening. The teams that struggled more were those who had been dedicated to set up/tear down. We tried to leverage their energy into new opportunities, but many felt like they had no purpose now—"Everything's already set up!" Some made the move to new opportunities, some didn't.

It was a thrilling Sunday in July 2006 when I walked onto the new campus of Thomas Road Baptist Church. Dr. Falwell had cast the vision of this day for many years, and now it was fulfilled. There was energy in the air with lots of celebration among the thousands who had gathered in the new worship center.

Except for one. In the sea of people, I ran into a familiar face, a precious widow, a sweet woman who had served for years in loving the children of Thomas Road. She loved her church, but she was overwhelmed by this new campus, this new direction. She stood there and cried and said, "I don't know if I like this. I don't know if I still fit." I took the next several minutes giving her a retraining pep talk. She needed to see that she still "fit," that her serving was more critical than ever to the new families and children pouring through the doors.

- Is your volunteer-vision clear? Are you ready to lead this serving family?
- Are you ready to connect people to the adventure of a lifetime?
- Will you coach them with all your heart, equipping and encouraging them in this kingdom work?

If so, accept these words from Paul on your leadership:

Serve wholeheartedly, as if you were serving the Lord, not men. (Eph. 6:7 NIV)

And we pray this in order that you may live a life worthy of the Lord and may please him in every way: bearing fruit in every good work, growing in the knowledge of God. (Col. 1:10 NIV)

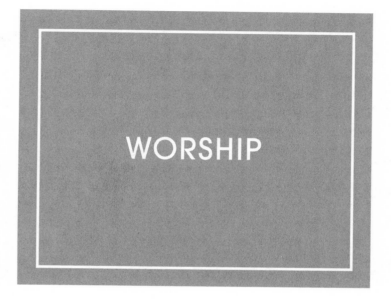

WORSHIP

CHAPTER 5

Innovate Worship

Utilizing diverse musical and cultural approaches
to discover new ways of genuinely experiencing
the awe of worship in our churches

by Charles Billingsley

The very term *innovate worship* carries with it the connotation that what we are doing at Thomas Road Baptist Church, by way of music, is ground-breaking. While I would love to say that is true—and in some ways, perhaps it is true—I really don't think we do much mechanically or musically that is, by and large, innovative. Rather, what we are doing is constantly learning what it means to have a fresh encounter with the presence of God through music and the experience of true worship. And when the presence of God begins to manifest itself, things tend to get real innovative, real fast.

I would like to begin by defining what I mean by "innovate worship." First, I want to tell you what this phrase does *not* mean.

It is not a style of music, nor a particular look, or feel or sound that exists in a worship service. Put simply, I see innovation in worship as a mechanism by which we can guide people into the inexpressible presence of God. That definition may seem elementary, but I see it as being a real concept that can greatly impact our churches. What pastor would not want to step into the pulpit after his people have just experienced a poignant worship service? Sadly, I see very few churches in our nation experiencing dynamic worship encounters with the true, living God in their services. My goal is to assist pastors and worship leaders worldwide in understanding the incredible potential that exists for powerful worship services among their own congregations.

Over the course of this chapter, I want to examine different approaches my staff and I take in preparing for our praise and worship services. I will also discuss some basic principles that I try to apply when planning and leading worship services. I certainly don't claim to be an authority, but I have found these principles to be helpful, on many occasions, as I attempt to escort believers into the realm of biblical worship. I want to urge readers to always bear in mind that even the best musicians and technical teams must still rely completely on the presence of God to experience true heaven-sent power in worship services. When we lean solely on our own talents and skills, we will always fall short of humbly and worshipfully approaching the throne of God.

Let's briefly outline some very important skills that every worship leader should have. Over the past sixteen years, I have had the privilege of traveling to many wonderful churches to sing. In fact, I've been to more than eighteen hundred churches. I have seen or participated in everything from Episcopalian weddings to evangelical stadium crusades. I have sung in venues ranging from backyard Bible clubs to the House of Blues in New Orleans to more Baptist churches than I could ever hope to recall. Every concert or worship service in which I have sung carries its own unique memory. It's funny how certain things that have happened over the course of my life often come to mind. I rely heavily on these memories because I have seen many innovations in worship that work and a few that have fallen short. And unfortunately I have had to learn the hard way about most everything I know. There have been times that I miserably failed to accomplish my goal of leading true worship in these events. But I must say that those failures certainly taught me valuable lessons regarding effective worship services. Even in failure, we have an opportunity to learn and grow.

So, utilizing my past experiences, both positive and negative in leading praise and worship services across America, I want to examine four key factors in becoming an effective worship leader.

1. Every worship leader must be a genuine worshiper. If we are going to be innovative and effective worship leaders, we must experience true worship, ourselves. It is imperative that we live lives above reproach that are blameless in the sight of God and man. We also must have routine periods of worship in our lives to continually prepare our hearts to lead worship encounters for others. This sounds very basic, I know, but you might be surprised at how few worship leaders follow this pattern. Here's an important fact: in Scripture, the term *worship* does not actually refer to music. It is a far more intense concept. Romans 12:1–2 speaks of presenting our bodies as living sacrifices. The apostle Paul says this is our spiritual act of worship. So we see that worship is not a song; it is not an instrument; it is not a voice; it is not a fad; and it is not an industry. It is a lifestyle. Each day, every worship leader must live purely for Jesus if he/she is going to have an impact with their congregation. How can we ever expect to lead our congregations into the presence of Almighty God if we are not regularly experiencing His presence in our own hearts and minds?

2. Every worship leader must understand his/her role. If we have been placed in the position of worship leader, it is a given that we must be a leader of people. We are, in many respects, a pastor to the flock of musicians in our care. We are accountants, with a budget. And in this role, we often have to be prepared to deal with conflict. Sometimes we must become counselors to temperamental singers. And we must occasionally make unpopular decisions.

We are also administrators of an office. Often, we find ourselves balancing a variety of roles: teacher, producer, director, counselor, and even janitor! On top of this, we, as worship leaders, must be the visionaries for the future of music and all things artistic for our churches. We must understand the needs of the people in our churches and then do our best, through Christ, to meet those needs and even take the worship experience beyond those needs. Of course, while we are wearing all these hats in our church role, we are also balancing our lives as spouses and parents.

3. Every worship leader must build a team. It can be extremely hard to play all these mentioned roles every week. That's why we shouldn't try to accomplish the task alone. In addition to constantly leaning on the Lord, I believe we must build an effective and spirit-filled team to help facilitate true worship every week. Of course, we all have our strengths and weaknesses. For instance, I am a much better platform person than I am an administrator. I am most comfortable standing before an audience, singing praises to God, or leading people in worship. Nevertheless, each Monday through Friday, I must play the role of administrator, with the help of a wonderful and selfless staff. Then on Sunday, I am in my real comfort zone on the platform. I say all this to encourage you to surround yourself with personnel and musicians that complement your weaknesses. If you are a strong acoustic guitarist, pray that God will send you a great pianist. If you are a great organizer and administrator, then surround yourself with people of musical vision and creative ideas. As worship leaders, we must also be willing to help others discover their most effective roles. I have learned that one of the truly wonderful things about the body of Christ is that each body part uniquely complements the other. There's no need for us to try to fill roles that God has not equipped us for or called us to. And as Pastor Jonathan Falwell always says, "It is amazing what we can accomplish when no one cares who gets the credit."

Innovative worship leading begins with the right team in place. Each team member must have strengths and skills the other team members don't have. At Thomas Road Baptist Church, we are blessed with many skilled musicians and excellent singers. I don't mind telling you that I am, by far, the least skilled musician on the team. That doesn't bother me. Scott Bullman, our worship choir director, is an incredibly skilled choral director, but he is also a wonderful counselor and listener. Linwood Campbell, an amazing pianist with perfect pitch, is also a strong arranger and conductor. Adam Lancaster is a superb musician with excellent taste and a real beat on modern culture, but he is also accomplished on a variety of instruments and is an excellent engineer. Rusty Goodwin, a fantastic singer, is also very gifted as an administrator and leader. I could go on and on, but I think you see the point. The best team is the one whose members' strengths complement the others' weaknesses. Even worship leaders at small churches can build effective worship teams by identifying the strengths and weaknesses of those who wish to serve.

4. Every worship leader must differentiate between being a music director and a worship leader. During the week, in our role as music director, we are involved in planning, rehearsing, preparing, organizing, and even agonizing over the Sunday worship service. I always look at this as what I sometimes call "time in the kitchen." We are busy working away at preparing a feast to be offered up to the Lord on Sunday. Then, when Sunday morning arrives, it is time to celebrate. I really try to make sure all the technical and mechanical issues are worked out well in advance so that Sunday is simply about worshipping Him without any detours. The Sunday service is the time to seek His face and His glory. I realize that rehearsal time can also turn into a sweet moment of praise. In fact, we have had many times like that. As worship leaders though, we are charged with ensuring that true praise and worship becomes a regular part of our churches' services. It is imperative that we develop sensitivity to the moving of the Spirit of God in our worship services on Sunday. Again, the challenge is to further develop in those areas in which we are not so strong and to surround ourselves with the right team to pick up where we fall short.

5. Every worship leader must lead worship. This sounds like a redundant statement, but I had to learn this the hard way. I began my worship-leading journey while I was a junior in college at Samford University in Birmingham, Alabama, at a small church-start called The Church at Brookhills. I was extremely green and really knew very little about music. But I loved the Lord, could carry a tune, and I wanted to serve. It was a fairly contemporary environment, so I would print our songs on little sheets of paper that went in the weekly bulletin for people to join along in times of singing. It was an enjoyable time, and every week was a huge learning experience for me.

One day particularly stands out. On this day the pastor very kindly said, "You know, Charles, I love your passion and your enthusiasm. You are like a puppy dog full of energy who will charge through a glass door just to get outside and run. Don't lose that!" Then he added, "But, Charles, don't get so wrapped up in your personal worship, that you forget to lead the people." This admonition stung a little, but I began to understand what he was trying to tell me. My problem was that I was getting completely carried away in a song that I loved, or one that I had written, and I would leave everybody else behind, so to speak. I would close my eyes and have a grand old time just lifting my heart to the Lord, but I was failing at engaging the congregation in corporate praise.

I have since learned that effective church worship is both corporate and individual. Corporate worship is when we gather together as believers to call upon the name of the Lord. Individual worship is that daily, personal quiet time before Him that sustains our hearts and nourishes our souls. Every believer needs both of these types of worship. It is subsequently imperative, as worship leaders, that we are able to distinguish between our personal encounter with the Lord and leading a body of believers into His presence. My number-one job when I stand before a congregation is to engage them in corporate worship. That means I can't close my eyes the whole service and pretend they are not there. It also means that I can't fill the service with songs nobody knows. (There's certainly nothing wrong with teaching new songs, but people can't worship through music when they regularly don't know the songs.) It also means that I can't run off and leave the musicians behind. I have done that too and it is very distracting to the worship experience.

Now, some congregations, like our student body at Liberty University, need very little direction by the worship leader to focus their mind's attention and their heart's affection on the Lord. They are passionate worshipers, and all I typically need to do is start the song. In fact, our worship leaders at Liberty lead from the dark. They call it "faceless worship." They don't want to draw unnecessary attention to themselves or the platform. I love this concept. And, in a congregation as engaged as the Liberty students, it works very well. However, with less engaged crowds, it takes quite a bit of work on the worship leaders' part to get people rightly focused. This requires a keen eye and open ears wherein we recognize how people are responding and we then react purposefully and accordingly.

To conclude this section, I want to say that I believe that every worship leader must learn to engage a congregation both "vertically" and "horizontally." By engaging them vertically, I mean focusing their minds and hearts on the Lord. Engaging a congregation horizontally simply refers to helping your congregation, music team, and tech team become more aware of how the Lord is moving in others around them. There is a difficult balance that I try to find each week. I depend on guidance from the Holy Spirit and my understanding in what the congregation needs to remain fully involved in corporate worship. I want to jointly be a Spirit-led and people-perceptive worship leader at all times. This is not easy, but it is important because my goal is to focus their minds and hearts in such a way that they begin to sense when the Holy Spirit is moving. Once this happens, it is incredible what takes place. We have had many moments like this at Thomas Road, and each time it happens, it deepens the hunger of the congregation, the musicians and me to dwell therein as long as we can. This sounds mysterious, I know, but *nothing* can replace the power of the Spirit of God moving in the room and changing lives. Sometimes we experience a still hush that fills the sanctuary. Other times it is a loud outburst of praise. But every time there is a power that is unexplainable in human terms.

So how do we regularly accomplish this? Obviously, it is the manifestation of the Holy Spirit that draws us into that moment. However, I believe there are some practical things we can do as worship leaders to create an environment conducive to the entire congregation responding to that manifestation.

I want to introduce you to four key words that I keep in the forefront of my mind when planning and implementing worship services. Again, I am not sure how truly innovative these concepts are, but these four words help me to stay on task and envision how I need to lead my congregation into God's presence, most effectively.

Focus

I have discovered that it is much easier to plan and lead worship services when there is a focus on a particular subject matter. Maybe the focus is on a certain biblical topic, such as holiness or forgiveness. Or perhaps the focus is built around a pastor's sermon topic. Other times it can be about an annual celebration such as Christmas or what we call our yearly "Sonrise Service," which celebrates the Risen Savior. Regardless of the subject, focusing the music and the worship time will help in terms of song choice and other elements, such as video, drama, or communion. It will also help to focus the hearts of your congregation.

There are several questions you can ask yourself in relation to focus and planning of worship services. Ask yourself these questions: "Who is here?" This might sound goofy, but I think many times we don't really look at the congregation we are leading. Are they connecting? Are they responding? Are they focusing on the Lord?

Another key question: "What is the goal?" I always try to begin the worship service with the end in mind. In fact, it is my goal to be at a place where we are so tuned in and sensitive to the Spirit of God that worshipers will actually move into a temperament of invitation even before our pastor, Jonathan Falwell, begins to preach.

Also ask yourself: "Is there a theme?" Even if I don't know my pastor's sermon topic (which is very rare), I typically choose a topic in which to focus the music. I always let the lyrics of the song—not its style—dictate whether or not I use it.

Flow

Worship services that have focus usually flow better. There are many elements involved in creating flow. I have discovered that, of all the important factors in our corporate worship times, flow is probably the hardest to accomplish. Making a service flow properly requires the active participation of all your musicians and technical people. Here are a few helpful items that can help your worship services flow.

- Use the same or relative keys between songs to enable ease of transition.
- Try common tone key changes for quick shifts to a new song.
- Stick with the theme. This helps if there is an awkward key change. You can briefly say something related to the theme to keep the people focused while the instrumentalists change keys.
- Try songs that match, in terms of tempo. This makes for an easy change of songs.
- Learn to recognize the difference between "dead time" and a holy hush. Usually this will be obvious by how the people are reacting to the service. I avoid dead time at all costs because, again, a congregation can become disengaged very quickly.

- Spend extra time in rehearsals, working out what will take place between songs and defining how you wish to move from one element in the service to the next. It should be smooth and seamless so it doesn't distract the focus of your people.
- Most importantly, work hand-in-hand with your sound and technical people to avoid odd microphone mishaps, feedback, or other problems. The audio engineers, video people, lighting technicians, IMAG operators, and any others involved in technical ministry should be as fully engaged as you are in every element of the service. They need to have a copy of the worship service outline, and it is imperative that the worship leader discuss every part of the service with them beforehand. There is nothing that will kill the flow of a worship service more quickly than a disengaged or an unprepared technical team.
- Invitation time is critical for flow. You may not do a walk-the-aisle invitation at your church, but even so, there is most likely some sort of "decision time" element at the end of the service. This is a crucial moment and it is very important that all your musicians and technical people are fully aware of how the Lord is moving. Train your team to follow your lead during times of invitation or end-of-service periods of spiritual reflection. Work out signals that are easy to read that allow you to communicate without words so that you are not distracting to the people who are doing business with God.
- Finally, frequently communicate with the pastor and understand his personality and preferences. Remember, the pastor is actually the true worship leader of the church and he probably has a good idea how he wants services to flow. So remain flexible in order to accommodate your pastor.

Flexibility

I am increasingly convinced that flexibility is more about attitude than skill. I also believe that flexibility is a learned trait. When you are blessed with a group of spiritually-minded people on your music and technical teams, those individuals will be willing to work with you when it comes to changing things "on the fly." Sometimes this is necessary in order to flow with how the Holy Spirit is moving in an individual service. At times it may become apparent that a song needs to be discarded or that another song should be quickly utilized instead of the one you are using. Perhaps a solo needs to be cut out or a Scripture reading needs to be added. While a well-thought-out worship service usually flows well, there will be times when change needs to happen—and happen quickly! If your team is flexible, this can take place without a hitch. I am very big on this because, as a worship leader, I am under the authority of my pastor who may often want to switch things around with little notice. Or, if something doesn't seem to flow right or feel right, I will change it or cut it myself. All of this is done for one reason: we are trying to ensure the experience of the congregation is a heart-lifting worshipful moment.

I have, on many occasions, had a service completely planned. It looked great on paper, but in all actuality, it was not what the Lord had in mind for that day. I am blessed to have a pastor who senses this as quickly as I do, and we are able to swiftly make appropriate changes from the platform. Here are a few ways in which you can build flexibility into your worship services.

- Surround yourself with flexible players, if possible. This is not easy to accomplish, especially in smaller congregations, because most musicians think in terms of notes and measures. Nevertheless, when you have a band or orchestra or just a single piano player who is flexible, they rely more on feeling and flow than measures and notes. This allows the worship leader to concentrate on engaging the people and hearing

direction from the Lord. If the leader feels like he/
she wants to add a chorus, it becomes no big deal. If
the leader senses he/she needs to skip a verse, again
there is no big deal. However, the more players that are
utilized in a worship service the harder flexibility is to
accomplish. If there is one area of our music at Thomas
Road Church in which I believe we are doing some truly
innovative things, it is here. We are orchestrating songs
with built-in flexibility and it greatly helps in the flow
of our worship.

- Make sure that you and your team actually know the
  songs. I realize with so many great worship songs and
  hymns available to use in our worship services, this can
  be difficult. But the better we know a song and the
  more the pianist or band or orchestra has played it, the
  easier it will be for you to lead it and the quicker the
  congregation will go from learning a song to actually
  worshipping through it.

- Have several songs in your memory banks that you can
  pull out and utilize at anytime. This is very helpful
  especially when it comes to an invitation time. If you
  put lyrics on a video screen and you use PowerPoint or
  a program like MediaShout, this also requires an IMAG
  or screen operator who is adapt at pulling up song lyrics
  quickly and smoothly. And when the screen operator
  actually knows the song too, that is wonderful.

- Move people around on a regular basis. One thing
  I recently learned at Thomas Road Church is that
  I never want our worship team to get too comfortable
  in one place because this begins to dig a rut. And a rut
  is nothing more than a grave with both ends knocked
  out. Our pastor's sermon series over the past several
  months have dictated the need for us to be flexible and
  mobile in terms of where people are set up every week.
  This was initially difficult to adjust to, but it has proven

to be very helpful in developing a flexible mind-set with our team. Now, about every six weeks or so, we have a totally different look on our platform. Even the congregation has gotten excited to see the change on a regular basis. And, believe it or not, it has made the congregation a more flexible group, as well.

- Bottom line: when you have flexibility in your worship services, it creates an unspoken energy and excitement in the air. It is as if you are suddenly coming to church with brand new expectations that the Holy Spirit will move on that day. Further, you and your team are ready for that moving of the Spirit. This leads to freedom and a revival-like atmosphere like few congregations have ever experienced.

Freedom

Focus begets flow. Flow begets flexibility. And flexibility begets freedom. Have you ever been in a worship service where there was no sense of freedom? Maybe the staff was so uptight and nervous about making a mistake that it led even the people in the pews to stiffen. Or maybe there was just no excitement in the air. I have never forgotten the words of one of my pastors, who said, "Never confuse reverence with rigor mortis!"

Once your congregation is experiencing freedom in your worship services, you will never want to return to a rigid service. I won't ever forget the first time I witnessed this at Thomas Road Church several years ago. I was singing a solo to a track. It was not a big, barn-burner song with ten key changes and a high C at the end, but rather a simple worship song that I had written with a few friends. Suddenly, there was an anointing on that song that I had never before sensed at Thomas Road. I reached the first chorus, and to my left about six rows back, a man stood up with his eyes closed and his hands pointed straight to the sky. He was worshipping freely and uninhibited amidst the stares of a few people near him. Then another man stood, followed by another. Then I saw my old friend Charlie Padgett stand. By the time I got to the bridge of the song, the entire congregation was standing in astounding reverent worship. Here is the best part: they were not standing because of some remarkable note I sang or some cool vocal lick. They were standing in free worship of the Lord Jesus Christ! It was, I believe, one of the first times I had ever experienced a moment like this that I can honestly say we were worshipping in spirit and in truth. Most wonderfully, it was not a moment manufactured by man. It just happened. And from that moment on, we have been on this incredible journey of discovering the wonder of worshipping in His presence. I hunger for it, and so does the church family at Thomas Road Church. The reason for this is that we have tasted and we have seen just a glimpse of the glorious power that His manifest presence brings. We want more of it! I learned that day that my job as a worship leader is not to whoop up a feeling, but simply to facilitate this freedom. Here are a few helpful ideas to create freedom in your worship services.

- Remember the little things. Simple acts like smiling from the platform, a humorous statement or a short time of audience fellowship in the midst of a song can revolutionize the response of the people to worship songs. It is really amazing how different the congregation sings when they are comfortable with their surroundings and each other. These little things can help relax an uneasy crowd. By the way, almost every crowd is uneasy, at first. Many times they don't know who they are sitting next to, or they are unfamiliar with a particular song, or there are things in their lives that are causing them to be uncomfortable in church. Whatever the case, when a worship leader confidently steps to the microphone with a smile and a purpose, the uneasiness usually subsides and people are well on their way to engaging in the worship experience.

Conversely, when the leader is nervous or distant, or the band is ill-prepared, or the choir isn't ready, or lyrics are consistently wrong on the video screens, the crowd responds accordingly.

- Use your personality as a worship leader to bring about freedom in a worship service. I have known some worship leaders who are blessed with high energy, humorous, magnetic personalities. But when they walk onto a platform, their personality suddenly and mysteriously turns wooden. Unfortunately their personality generates a similar aloof response with their congregations. So be real and be yourself. Your congregation is smart and can easily smell a fake. If you have a quiet or impassive personality, don't try to force yourself into being something you are not (although you might try to somewhat ramp up your energy without becoming phony). If you have a bubbly, free-spirited personality, use that energy from the platform. I have learned that congregations eventually take on the personality of their leaders.

- Use planned spontaneity. I do this all the time. What I mean is, plan some points in the worship service that will appear spontaneous, even though they are not. Of course, I let the instrumentalists know that I am considering adding a chorus or something like that, so they are ready when I actually do it. This keeps the worship service feeling fresh and exciting and it really engages the people because they won't feel as if you are just going through the motions on another Sunday morning.

- Use creative elements like drama or video to enhance the freedom in your worship services. These are powerful mediums to get across an idea or theme. When placed properly in the service, they can produce a huge response of praise from the people. For instance,

I introduced a song a few months before Dr. Falwell died titled, "We Will Remember." It is a wonderful tune by Tommy Walker. At the time I just thought it was a great song and I wanted our people to learn it. Then on May 15, 2007, everything changed. Dr. Falwell passed away and no one really felt like singing anything. Two months later, on our church's Anniversary Sunday (July 1), we prepared a video honoring Dr. Falwell. And during the video, we sang "We Will Remember." Suddenly that song took on new meaning and people were responding powerfully to its lyrics and its melody. The hearts of the people were resonating with the lyrics, and it became a powerful moment of worship and thanksgiving. In fact, we named it our theme song for 2007.

Young and Old Worshipping Together

These are just a few ideas for you when it comes to planning your worship services. But I think these topics bring up a few more questions. For example, what does "innovate worship" sound like? What does it look like? Should it involve a choir and orchestra? Do I cater to the church's younger members because they are the future of the church, or do I indulge the preferences of the older members because they have been here so long and largely pay the bills? All of these are valid questions that I run into quite frequently. In fact, as the worship leader of a large church, I have a huge, diverse congregation for which I am responsible. Let's examine some of these issues.

1. **What does innovate worship sound like?** Honestly I don't think there is a particular sound or style to it, even though I should note that some songs carry a special anointing. I believe true innovative worship is the same kind of worship Paul refers to in Ephesians 5: psalms, hymns, and spiritual songs. However, I also believe that resonating worship occurs when the congregation

and music team gain a true understanding of biblical worship. We must teach our members that worship goes far beyond a song. Worship is a lifestyle and should infiltrate every avenue of our lives. Worship is what we were created to do and we must help our congregations understand that worship is as much a part of their lives on Monday morning as it is on Sunday morning. Once they really begin to grasp this, the issue of style starts to fade.

2. **What does innovate worship look like?** Again, I don't think it has a particular appearance. I have experienced powerful worship services in churches with huge choirs and orchestras, and I have participated in services equally powerful when all you could hear was an acoustic guitar. It is not the instrumentation or the size that is the real issue. The true concern is that we are seeking God's presence. I must say that I see in some churches a movement away from relying on God to move among us. Tragically the utensils of worship take precedence over the true worship experience. These churches tend to rely on technical fireworks or human performance over pure quests for God's presence. I call them "production churches." I am convinced that a great many worship services could go on for months at a time at these types of churches before anyone ever realized that there is a living God who would like to take part. We must remember why we gather to worship Him! We bless Him with our absolute praise. If we are not careful, we will get so caught up in producing a great show that we will fail to humbly bow before Almighty God. Don't get me wrong; I understand the need for a technically sound production. Thomas Road Church is on live television every Sunday and in the homes of 2.4 billion people around the world. It is imperative that things run smoothly. However, we are discovering that hurting people are way more

interested in authentic worship than silky shows. If people notice our arts more than our hearts, something is out of order.

3. **Does innovation in worship involve a choir or orchestra or praise band or praise singer?** The answer is, yes. Innovate worship involves as many people as possible. I am a firm believer that, as worship leaders, our primary function outside of leading the congregation in worship is to raise up worshipers within the body. I can't do this if I limit the involvement of our people to just a select few. Obviously, there are those on our team that are more talented than others, but everybody has a place. I am much more interested in the motive and the passion and the heart of our members than I am about their talent. I read a long time ago that ninety percent of what people learn and remember is not what they hear, but what they see. I want people on our worship team to help our congregation see Jesus. I can always find a decent singer. I am on the lookout for individuals who are consumed by the love of Christ and not interested in personal gain or about who is getting more solos than the other person. When I find true worshipers, I am immediately drawn to them because they have a deeper understanding of biblical, lifestyle worship. Sure, we struggle at Thomas Road Church because we are trying to maintain a certain standard while also utilizing everyone who wants to serve. It is not an easy balance to find, but with the help of a great staff and much prayer, we work through each situation one person at a time. One thing is sure: I will always find a way to involve a passionate worshiper.

4. **What about the people in church who prefer one style over another?** This actually includes all of us because we all have preferences. I like black gospel music and don't particularly care for southern gospel. I like pop and some country, but I'm not moved by rap or heavy R&B. I like

light blues and light rock, but I don't care for bluegrass
and honky-tonk. I think you get the picture. Most every
congregation has within it believers of all ages, races,
and backgrounds, so it is not surprising that this is a
common issue. Nevertheless, it is our duty to understand
the culture in which our local church exists and to meet
the diverse needs through our song choices and worship
service planning. If you are in a rural area in southern
Georgia, there is a good chance your folks respond well
to southern gospel. If you are in Southern California, it is
probable that your congregation is going to favor a more
contemporary approach. Worship leaders must meet these
unique areas with song choices that fit the area, while
also attempting to occasionally stretch the congregation's
tastes. Once you have a good understanding of where
your congregation sits musically, it is then your duty to
bring them into a deeper understanding of true worship.
Most churchgoers simply know what they like and what
they don't like. We must help them understand, from a
biblical standpoint, that worship goes way beyond their
partiality to a certain musical style and reaches down
into the very core of who they are in Christ. Do we really
think that God prefers one style over another? Of course
not! I think many American believers are going to be
shocked to find they are sharing their eternal home in
heaven with people from Africa, China, India, Mexico,
and the rest of the nations. Do you think that the people
in Africa like southern gospel? The point is this: style
should never even be an issue. Yet, church after church
has split over this very thing. I believe bodies of believers
who get hung up on issues as small as this are caught
up in a carnality that goes much deeper. They have a
fundamental misunderstanding of biblical worship. When
we place one style over the other, we are assigning a
moral value to a personal preference. And it is usually the

worship leader who ends up receiving the brunt of the blame. Again, it is our job to teach our people a greater understanding of biblical worship. If we inform them correctly and introduce new songs wisely with a gentle approach, the great majority of our people will actually appreciate the change.

The Balance of Worship

I always do my best to incorporate all styles in worship, although I haven't tried rap yet and have no ability for it. (However, we sometimes use rap at Liberty University because it is a highly popular art form among our culturally diverse student body.) I do my best to use psalms, hymns, and spiritual songs in every service. Naturally, while I have my preferences, I work very hard at achieving a fair and unbiased approach when choosing songs. Some people call this "blended worship." I call it balanced. I got that term from a friend named Simeon Nix who is a worship leader in Florida. I love the word *balanced* because it captures the constituency of most congregations. We have everything from eight- to-eighty-year-old worshipers in our services. I try to incorporate as many elements and styles as I can in every service in order to engage as many as I can into worship.

So I have essentially set the style issue aside, in this regard. I no longer plan worship services around the preferences of the people. Instead, I plan worship services centered on the goal that *all* of our members are experiencing the presence of God. Further, I trust the Lord to guide me in my choice of songs. When I started doing this, the music didn't change much, but my motives changed immensely. The people began to sense this and, believe it or not, their motives began to change, as well. There is nothing more beautiful than seeing a congregation move from a position of "what can I get today?" to the passion of "what can I give today?" Remember, it is not about us, but about Him!

Therefore, to truly worship God and to lead worship

effectively, it is important that we understand five basic principles. I learned this from Vernon Whaley, the director of our Center for Worship at Liberty University. It is inspired from 2 Chronicles 5–7.

1. Our success in public worship is a direct reflection of our commitment to worshipping together in unity. We must get along with each other.
2. Our success for genuine worship replicates our heart motive for worship. The only one deserving credit for what God has done is God Himself. At Thomas Road Church, we have come to depend on the individual and corporate policy of "Not I, but Christ."
3. Our success for acceptable worship is not dependant upon ability or skill. No one is indispensable. God can do quite well without us.
4. Our success for holy worship displays our own personal desire to see the glory of God revealed. God's desire for all nations is likewise that His glory is revealed.
5. Our success in leading worship is in direct proportion to the presence of God upon our own lives. We cannot expect to lead anyone in worship if we haven't been in His presence ourselves.

I hope that I have been able to identify for you the motivating factors of "innovatechurch." We see that it is the engaging of the people of God into the presence of God. It is not determined by preference, hindered by style, built on instrumentation, or created by performance. Rather, it is reliant upon the manifestation of the Holy Spirit and it requires a worship team that is sensitive to how the Spirit is moving. It is nothing new, as it has been happening among believers for thousands of years. But, strangely enough, it has been missing in many congregations. My prayer is that we will all become a greater part of the worship revival that is sweeping the nations. I pray that we will set aside our musical and cultural differences and instead learn what it is to simply dwell in His presence. It reminds me of a song I recorded a few years ago that is titled "In Your Presence."

> In Your presence
> I can hear You.
> Everything around me
> Is silenced by Your voice.
>
> In Your presence
> I draw near to
> The things that really matter
> And are closest to Your heart.
> I find them there . . . there in Your presence.

It is in His presence that souls are saved, marriages are mended, and lives are changed. That is where I want to be. That is where we must lead our people.

He is worthy!

DISCIPLESHIP

CHAPTER 6

What Is God's Will for My Life? Disciple!

by Rod Dempsey

Jesus had just died. The disciples were dazed and confused. They believed that Jesus would deliver them from the Roman oppression. They also believed that they were on their way to something big. But the awful events of the last few days were just too much to comprehend: Jesus' arrest in the garden; the trial in Pilate's courtyard; the scourging by the Roman guards. Jesus was crucified right before their eyes. What were they going to do now? All of them were nervous, and some even went into hiding. They were overwhelmed with doubts and fear. Matthew probably said he was going back to his job of collecting taxes. Most of the rest said they were going back to fishing. The excitement they had known by traveling with Jesus and witnessing His miracles had quickly faded. The dream was, in their minds, over.

That is, until the third day. First, the women came running to the disciples with an incredible story. Then the disciples went to the tomb and found that Jesus wasn't there. Then He appeared to them out of nowhere like a ghost. But He was no ghost. The disciples believed that He did actually live, while some of them doubted. But they eventually all came to believe because they could see that He was fully alive. Jesus' final appearance was full of encouragement and instruction to His friends. He told them to go and make disciples of the entire world. They had their marching orders, but they were also told to wait until the Spirit of Promise had come. Jesus was about to inaugurate a new age with the coming of the Spirit. So they started praying for forty days. And then came Pentecost! The disciples were transformed from fearful to fearless; from aimless to having purpose. They decided to obey their Master no matter what the cost. They also decided to follow and accomplish His plan, and by the time they arrived at Ephesus (see Acts 17:6) they were regarded as those people who "turned the world upside down."

InnovateChurch is about being a passionate follower of Jesus and being passionately involved in His kingdom. You cannot be a passionate follower of Jesus without being intimately involved in His mission. That mission is carried out in and through the local church. This chapter will tackle what it means to be a disciple (What is God's will for my life?), while the next chapter will examine the process of discipleship (What is God's will for my church?). Let's begin with an analysis of some of the challenges facing an individual who desires to "come after" Christ.

There are distractions facing a person who wants to be like Jesus. Apart from a personal decision and an intentional plan to develop as a believer, there are many decoys and temptations designed to either lure us from our faithfulness or to actually challenge that very faith. They include: moral relativism (evidenced by political correctness and the disappearance of absolutes), the proliferation of Internet pornography (evidenced by the epidemic of Christians in bondage to it), the breakdown of the family through divorce (evidenced by the number of homes, even Christian homes, without fathers), materialism and greed (evidenced by the often trivial giving patterns of church members) and the diluting of the gospel (evidenced by the number of churches that no longer believe in the divine inspiration and inerrancy of Scripture).

On top of these obstacles, we also face an increasingly hostile and anti-Christian environment. Across our nation we see public school Bible clubs challenged in courts, school choirs refused the right to sing Christmas carols, high school kids sent home because they wear pro-life T-shirts, Ten Commandments monuments and other Christian symbols removed from public places, and churches facing discriminatory zoning laws, to name just a few examples we are seeing.

However, even though the world is becoming ever more unwelcoming to the gospel, it is imperative that Christians remain true to their faith and committed to being bold apologists for Christ. We must not grow weary in well doing. We need to look to Hebrews 12:3: "For consider Him who endured such hostility from sinners against Himself, so that you won't grow weary and lose heart." God is our shield against discouragement.

In the first century, Peter, shortly after Jesus had died, boldly declared, "I'm going fishing" (John 21:3). Several disciples decided to go with him. We see that Peter's confusion and discouragement soon became too great to go forward so he decided to go back. We can see the attitudes of many Christians in Peter's actions. They face some discouragement of faith and they are soon saying, "I'm not sure about all this religious stuff. I am going back to what I know." By doing so, they put the things of the world ahead of the things of God. The famous Russian author Leo Tolstoy put it this way: "Everybody thinks of changing the world and no one thinks of changing himself."[1]

The way to reach the world with the gospel is for the gospel to fully reach the individual disciple. Twentieth-century psychologist Abraham Maslow said, "What a man can be, a man must be."[2] The church must continue to hone its efforts to ensure that the gospel is being presented in the most effective ways. The world is growing at an exponential rate and only similarly exponential strategies, those that involve the development of the total person, will most effectively work. The solution to the dilemma of reaching the total world lies in the reaching of the total person and unlocking his or her "kingdom potential." When every disciple is fully developed to his or her potential, reaching the world is then a result of obedience to the Great Commission. To create that type of disciple, we must first begin with a clear definition of what a disciple looks like.

The starting point, for becoming a disciple of Jesus, is to examine the Scriptures and see what the characteristics of a first-century disciple was. We may then draw from those passages bedrock principles regarding the development of a disciple. Further, from these principles, we need to create a working definition for the term *disciple*. It's been said, "If you aim at nothing you will hit it every time." Often times, churches seem to be trying to make disciples, but they are not clear on what a disciple actually looks like. In seminary, my homiletics professor put it this way: "Mist in the pulpit is fog in the pew." If we are not clear on the product, the process is hopelessly shrouded. As a result we are not producing disciples who shake the world; we are rather producing disciples who are being shaken by the world's influence. This is why, according to all of the statistics and trends, the average person in the church is indistinguishable from the average person in the world. We cannot reach the world when the world is dictating and defining the terms.

Let's take a look at the Scriptures and extract some core principles for the term *disciple* and then we will form a definition from the principles. The word *disciple* or *disciples* is used 266 times in the New Testament, with the vast majority of the occurrence recorded in the Gospels. Becoming a disciple requires that a person be disciplined in spiritual habits, as well as disciplined in purpose. The Epistles emphasize a relational community where disciples are developed in the context of a body of believers. They discover and use their spiritual gifts to love and serve each other, as well as nonbelievers. Disciples are developed as the body grows in maturity and as each part does its work (see Eph. 4:16). However, the clear call of Jesus, in the Gospels, to come and follow Him cannot be ignored. Jesus clearly identifies the marks of a disciple in the Gospel accounts and we need to start there. Here are the main passages related to being a disciple, as set forth by Jesus Himself.

Ten Key Facets of a Disciple

1. A disciple is someone who seriously considers the cost before following Christ. Luke 14:28: "For which of you, wanting to build a tower, doesn't first sit down and calculate the cost to see if he has enough to complete it?" This verse makes it clear that, before a person decides to follow Jesus, he or she must calculate the cost of following Christ. For the true disciple, it will only cost you your life, your body, your possessions, and your future. In short, it will cost you everything. God's plan and God's will cost Jesus His life; it cannot cost His followers anything less.

2. A disciple is someone who is totally committed to Christ. Jesus is first priority. Consider the following verse from Luke 14:26: "If anyone comes to Me and does not hate his own father and mother, wife and children, brothers and sisters—yes, and even his own life—he *cannot* be My disciple" (emphasis added). The term *hate* in this verse is a comparative term. Our love for Christ is so great, so consuming, that in comparison it feels like hatred (disdain) for others. Jesus said it this way in Matthew 6:33, "But seek first the kingdom of God and His righteousness, and all these things will be provided for you." This means that Jesus is first in our lives. This type of commitment is evidenced by a statement like this: "I will go anywhere and do anything that He asks of me."

3. A disciple is someone who is willing to carry his or her individual burden to sacrifice for Christ and His cause.

Consider Luke 14:27: "Whoever does not carry his own cross and come after Me cannot be My disciple" (NASB). Much has been written and discussed about what it means to "carry your cross." In a nutshell, it means that the disciple of Jesus will be called upon to lay down his life (his desire for self-direction and determination) and to surrender his will to the will of the Master. The kingdom of God is not advanced on a nine-to-five schedule. You cannot serve someone without eventually surrendering your will to the person you serve. Consider Luke 17:10, where Jesus says, "In the same way, when you have done all that you were commanded, you should say, 'We are good-for-nothing slaves; we've only done our duty.'" Obedience to the point of sacrifice, if called upon, is part of the commitment.

4. A disciple is someone who is willing to give up all earthly possessions. Luke 14:33: "So then, none of you can be My disciple who does not give up all his own possessions" (NASB). Again, we see the call to totally abandon any and all ownership to possessions. Jesus put it this way in Matthew 6:24: "No one can be a slave of two masters, since either he will hate one and love the other, or be devoted to one and despise the other. You cannot be slaves of God and of money." In the same passage, Jesus said this: "Where your treasure is, there your heart will be also" (v. 21). This doesn't mean that to be a disciple a person must take a vow of poverty, but the disciple must be "poor in spirit" and be willing to surrender all possessions if the Master asks.

5. A disciple is someone who continues in God's Word and experiences the freedom in Christ. John 8:31–32: "If you continue in My word, you really are My disciples. You will know the truth, and the truth will set you free." The Word of God is "living and active." It has the ability to "transform our minds" and our lives if we will read it,

study it, memorize it, and meditate in it on a consistent basis. The Word can set us free from the lies of the enemy and it can empower us to overcome the fiery darts of our adversary. If we don't continue in the Word, we are wide open to deception, discouragement, and even defeat. One cannot be a disciple without an aggressive commitment to consume and obey the Scriptures. As we drink in the Word of God, it has the power to transform our minds and when our minds are transformed then we can experience the good, acceptable, and perfect will of God.

6. A disciple is one who genuinely loves other believers. John 13:35: "By this all people will know that you are My disciples, if you have love for one another." If you don't love other believers, you don't know the God of love. That is the call and the challenge of Jesus in the upper room discourse, when He called His disciples together and told them to "love one another." The great twentieth-century theologian Francis Schaeffer observed that our love for one another should be so strong that it would unite believers to the point that their unity would spark the world to believe that Jesus was sent by God. The modern-day disciple must be committed to loving God, loving our neighbor, and loving our brothers and sisters in Christ. When we love like this, there is no argument that can stand against this force.

7. A disciple is one who abides in Christ, prays, bears fruit, and glorifies God. John 15:5, 7–8: "I am the vine, you are the branches; he who abides in Me and I in him, he bears much fruit, for apart from Me you can do nothing. If you abide in Me, and My words abide in you, ask whatever you wish, and it will be done for you. My Father is glorified by this, that you bear much fruit, and so prove to be My disciples" (NASB). When we abide in Christ, we know His will and ask for His will and it will be done. As a result, fruit will be produced for this type of

disciple and God will be glorified. John 15 is the clearest explanation of life as a follower of Christ. This passage should be the normative experience for the modern-day disciple. It is the clearest explanation of life in the kingdom as a disciple.

8. A disciple is one who is full of the Holy Spirit. Acts 13:52: "And the disciples were filled with joy and the Holy Spirit." Part of the fruit of abiding in Christ is the fruit of the Spirit, which is love, joy, peace, patience, kindness, goodness, faithfulness, gentleness, and self-control. The other part of fruitfulness is fruit that comes from serving and using your spiritual gift(s). John 15 says that a disciple should bear much fruit in his character and fruit in his actions. The Holy Spirit was sent by Jesus to "be with us" and to "guide us in all things." In order to fully follow Christ, we need to be full of the Holy Spirit, who will guide us into the path of obedience and fruitfulness and, ultimately, to joy.

9. A servant is one who obediently follows the desires of the Master. Matthew 26:19: "The disciples did as Jesus had directed them and prepared the Passover." Immediate and complete obedience is a hallmark of a disciple. Do you realize that it is impossible to ever say, "No, Lord"? You see, the moment you say "no," He is no longer the Lord. The Gospels portray following God as being a member in His kingdom. As loyal subjects in His kingdom, our job is to follow the King, to go wherever and do whatever He says. Many times we approach the kingdom of heaven in a casual "take it or leave it" manner. The parable of the talents and the parable of the minas make it very clear that one day the Master will return and call His servants into account. In order to hear from Him, "Well done, good and faithful servant," we must understand and assume the role of a servant. You cannot be rewarded by the Master if you have not obeyed the wishes of the Master.

10. A servant is one who is intimately involved in the mission of Jesus to make disciples. Matthew 28:16, 18–20: "The 11 disciples traveled to Galilee, to the mountain where Jesus had directed them. Then Jesus came near and said to them, 'All authority has been given to Me in heaven and on earth. Go, therefore, and make disciples of all nations, baptizing them in the name of the Father and of the Son and of the Holy Spirit, teaching them to observe everything I have commanded you. And remember, I am with you always, to the end of the age.'" These were some of the last words spoken by Jesus to His disciples before He ascended back into heaven. They must be carefully studied and diligently observed. A careful study of this passage yields: one command, three participles, and one promise. The command verb (in the imperative) is "make disciples." Whatever else we are involved in as followers of Christ, we must be involved in His mission. We cannot, as disciples, look at the person of Christ and respond to the person of Christ without responding to the mission of Christ. We will look at this passage in detail in the next chapter, but suffice it to say, this is the most important passage on the mission of the disciple and the church in the New Testament. It must be obeyed on an individual and corporate level.

These were the principles that clearly identified the first-century disciple. Can you imagine the wonder and amazement of the first disciples as they heard the Master identify the cost of following Him? What is your reaction when you read the words of Jesus as He explains the cost of discipleship? Hopefully, as you read these verses and the principles, your heart is stirred to accept Jesus' simple challenge of "follow Me." This challenge is clear and simple, but the cost is, when examined more closely, quite great. As you examine the cost of Jesus' call, and as you understand the nature and love of God, you come to realize that Jesus can and should be trusted, as no other should be trusted. Living in full trust of Jesus as our Lord is really the only way to live.

InnovateChurch is about (1) empowering disciples to discover God's plan for their lives and (2) discovering what God wants His disciples to do within His church. Starting from the Scriptures, and extracting the principles within, we can begin to see that the way of a disciple is challenging, but distinctively rewarding. Jesus said in John 10:10, "I have come that they may have life and have it in abundance."

We cannot ignore or gloss over the importance of starting with the Scriptures when defining a disciple. From the Scriptures, we can discover guiding principles that will help us create a definition for a modern-day disciple. And that definition must come from biblical principles in order to capture the image that God has in mind for a Christ follower.

Three Principles of Christian Disciples

1. Sacrificial

He or she has made a decision to submit to Christ and surrender their will and to follow Christ no matter the cost. The starting point of this commitment is salvation. After salvation, this person has seriously examined the cost and is willing to abandon family and possessions for the Master, if need be. This disciple is also willing to take up his or her cross and follow Christ to the ends of the earth. This sacrifice means we may be called to surrender our time, energy, body, and future plans. "Not I, but Christ" is not a motto, but a way of life. Submission to Christ and His plan is the highest goal for the modern-day disciple.

2. Relational

He or she understands that love is the hallmark of followers of Christ. If I love God, I will subsequently want to spend time with Him and His children. Love for God, love for neighbor, and love for other disciples is a very important part of the value system of a disciple. He or she will set aside time to be with other Christians for spiritual nourishment and encouragement, while also serving the body by discovering their spiritual gifts and using those gifts to serve Christians and non-Christians. The local church is the focal point for this relational community and service. A church that is innovative will prioritize the development of believers in community. Loving God and loving people is not only a consistent passion, but a consistent practice.

3. Transformational

He or she understands that the purpose of spiritual growth is directed toward becoming like Christ in word, thought, attitude, and action. Habits such as Bible study, journaling, Scripture memorization, meditation, silence, solitude, prayer, fasting, and giving are all means to an end. They connect us to the grace of God, and through the grace of God we are transformed into the image of Christ. As we become like Christ in character, we also become committed to the cause of Christ. Being should lead to doing. The disciple is transformed in their character and calling. The apostle Paul, in Philippians chapter three, wanted to know Christ, the fellowship of His sufferings, and the power of His resurrection. He wanted to have an intellectual and experiential knowledge of Christ. But he also wanted to "press on" and accomplish the work that he was called to do. The transformation that we are talking about for the disciple connects them to the person of Christ and connects them to the mission of Christ as well. The individual disciple discovers, develops, and uses his or her gift for the kingdom of God. You cannot be a follower of the person of Christ without being a follower of the mission of Christ.

From these three principles—Sacrificial, Relational, and Transformational—we can begin to develop a definition that will help to de-mystify what a disciple looks like. Then can we begin to design an organic process for disciple making. Here is my definition for a person who would follow Jesus: *A disciple is a person who has trusted Christ for salvation and has surrendered completely to Him. He or she is committed to practicing the spiritual disciplines in community and developing to their full potential for Christ and His mission.*

Now let's see if these three concepts are included in this definition.

Sacrificial: The person has not only come to the place where they have accepted the sacrifice of Christ, but he or she has *surrendered* to the rule and reign of Christ, as well. I was just nine years old when I accepted Christ as my Savior; but it wasn't until I was nineteen that I completely surrendered to God's will in my life. I was saved, but I wasn't "work[ing] out [my] own salvation with fear and trembling" (Phil. 2:12). I was not "applying diligence" and adding to my faith and, as a result, I was not useful or fruitful for the King or the kingdom (see 2 Pet. 1:1–10 NASB). At age nineteen, I made a statement to Christ to this effect: "Lord, I will go anywhere and do anything You tell me." I completely surrendered to Him as the ruler in my life. The disciple will not only yield to the person of Christ for salvation, he or she will submit to the plan of Christ, as well.

Relational: Hebrews 10:24–25 says that we should "be concerned about one another in order to promote love and good works, not staying away from our meetings, as some habitually do, but encouraging each other, and all the more as you see the day drawing near." From this passage, we see that we are to be pursuing Christ and serving Christ in the community of other believers. We are saved to serve! The book of Acts records the habits and practices of the early church, showing that they met together in the temple and "from house to house." This group of believers was committed to carrying out the teachings and mission of Christ in their community. In Acts 2:42–47, we have the clearest example of what the early church did. They were committed to the Word of God, fellowship, prayer, the needs of others, and praising God. As a result, the Bible says they had "favor with all the people." All this effort was done in a community of believers.

Transformational: God's goal for our lives is that each of us would bring the maximum amount of glory to Him. This is called the sum of all theology; we exist to bring God glory. And we bring glory to God, individually, by developing into His image and accomplishing His desires. We develop in community by discovering and using our spiritual gifts to serve the body and our fellow man. The church that equips the saints to do the "work of service" (see Eph. 4:12 NASB) will see individuals transformed into the image of Christ. When we reach our full potential in Christ, we will bear fruit and we bring God glory. John 15:8 says, "My Father is glorified by this, that you bear much fruit, and so prove to be My disciples" (NASB). To be an innovative church, we must start the innovation process with the individual disciple.

The early church made disciples, in part because they had the words of Jesus still ringing in their ears. In order to make disciples today, we must go back to the Scriptures and spend enough time in them so that the words of Jesus also begin to echo and resonate in our ears and then in our actions. Jesus said in John 10:27, "My sheep hear My voice." Can you hear the call of the Master to follow Him?

To become a disciple, you must answer this question: "What is God's will for my life?" To become an innovative church and pursue the process of discipleship, you must then answer another question: "What is God's will for my church?" That is the subject we examine in the next chapter.

Notes

1. http://wikiquote.org/wiki/Leo_Tolstoy.
2. http://www.brainyquote.com/quotes/authors/a/abraham_maslow. html.

CHAPTER 7

What Is God's Will for My Church? Discipleship!

by Rod Dempsey

Peter and the disciples were huddled together in an upper room in Jerusalem. They were certain about the death of Jesus, but now they were uncertain about their future because Jesus had told them not to move forward with the mission until they had received the Spirit. They had been praying nonstop for forty days when they suddenly heard a noise. It sounded like a tornado and the rushing wind blew right into the room where they were praying. Everyone saw "tongues of fire." And they began to speak in languages unknown to them, but known to others. Since it was the Day of Pentecost, thousands of pilgrims from all over the world were in Jerusalem. To their amazement, they could miraculously understand the different languages being spoken by the disciples. They were curious as to how this could be happening and they were equally curious as to what it all meant. Finally Peter, the impulsive disciple, arose to explain that what they were witnessing was the fulfillment of the prophet Joel, who said in the last days the Spirit of God would be poured out upon His people (see Joel 2:28–32). Peter explained that they were all witnesses of a new movement of God in their midst (see Acts 2:22). The command to take the gospel to the world now seemed like it might be a possibility.

Peter then did something really amazing. He began preaching a message that told all the listeners assembled there that they killed Jesus. What a bold transformation! This is the same disciple who, in the garden when Jesus was arrested, denied Jesus three times. The third time he had to emphasize that he did not know the man with a loud curse (see Matt. 26:74). The same man who didn't want to risk his life when Jesus was arrested was now laying his life on the line for this Man that he swore that he didn't even know. The amazing transformation in Peter was so complete that it is reported in history that he was ultimately crucified upside down.[1] The transformation was powerful in the person of Peter, but the transformation did not just affect his character—it affected his entire course of life. "Being" leads to "doing."

It is fascinating to note that Jesus chose Peter to bring the first message of the church age. It was in a conversation between Jesus and Peter that we see the first mention, uttered by Jesus, of the word "church" (Matt. 16:18). The occasion was Peter's declaration that Jesus was the "Messiah." In response to Peter's proclamation, Jesus replied: "I also say to you that you are Peter, and on this rock I will build My church, and the forces of Hades will not overpower it." It almost seems that the conversation about the church between Jesus and Peter in Matthew 16 is not complete until Peter's sermon in the second chapter of Acts. In this passage, we see Peter preaching the first message wherein a mob responded to the invitation and the church age (foretold in Matt. 16) was born.

The Purpose of the Church

The word *church* simply means a gathering of "called out ones."[2] Christians are called out of the world while being called to a Savior who has a mission for them. The church is a fulfillment of the kingdom and the kingdom is a fulfillment of the mission of God; the mission of God springs from His nature and love. John 3:16 says it best: "For God so loved the world, that He gave His only begotten Son, that whoever believes in Him shall not perish, but have eternal life" (NASB). God sent His Son on a mission to save the world. He accomplished His mission and now He asks us to finish the mission: "As the Father has sent Me, I also send you" (John 20:21). The church exists to win people to Christ, help them grow in their faith and then send them out to participate in the mission of winning the entire world. The process of growing them in their faith and sending them is called discipleship, and it is God's will for every church.

Now it has been two thousand years since the early church began the task of winning and discipling the world. The church has, of course, faced many challenges during this time, including: persecution; doctrinal heresies; the Dark Ages; and attempts to dilute the power and meaning of the gospel. In addition, the church has also faced challenges related to the understanding of what it is supposed to be doing. Some church leaders think they should be primarily showing love to the world, while others believe they should be condemning and criticizing the world, as part of their primary focus. Some churches adhere to the belief that they should be like the world and have become barely distinguishable from the world. The teaching of Jesus to be "in the world, but not of the world" (see John 17:11–16) is, of course, easier said than done. It is apparent to the casual observer that the interpretation of what the church should be doing is not as clear as one might think. Therefore, the first place to start with any attempt at discovering the will of God for the church is to study, interpret and apply the Word of God in relation to the church. Once we have discovered what the Scriptures say regarding discipleship, we may move on to develop principles for the church. From these principles, we create a definition for discipleship. As I noted in the earlier chapter, defining "disciple" is discovering God's will for my life. Defining "discipleship" is discovering God's will for my church.

And just like my previous chapter in this book, I want to follow a similar approach to defining what discipleship looks like. First, let's examine the Scriptures, then we will extract the principles and finally we will create a working definition for discipleship. Then we will illustrate and explain how a local church can begin to pursue the Great Commission in this context.

The Great Commandment

The first passage is called the "Great Commandment" and it is found in Matthew 22:36–40. As is so often the case, the occasion of Jesus' teaching is a question: "Teacher, which commandment in the law is the greatest?" And Jesus said to him, "Love the Lord your God with all your heart, with all your soul, and with all your mind." He went on to add, "This is the greatest and most important commandment." The second commandment is: "Love your neighbor as yourself." This passage contains many things to consider for the church that is seeking to "make disciples." From this passage, we see that the greatest command in the Law is to love God with all one's heart, soul, and mind. More than six hundred laws and statutes were essentially reduced to two: love God and love your neighbor. This means that Christian discipleship must be about helping people grow in their love and respect for God so that they can effectively witness to others. The scope of this love should be all encompassing, incorporating our total heart, soul, and mind in devotion to godly service.

The second part of this Great Commandment is similar to the first in that it revolves around love, but here is directed toward loving people. In order to properly love God we must be involved in showing and expressing that love to our neighbors. Jesus explained in the parable of the Good Samaritan that the way we show love to our neighbor is by meeting their needs, especially when others have bypassed this calling. The greatest and most pressing need that people have is to come into a right relationship with God. Therefore, the first step in Christian discipleship is to develop people who passionately love God and, in turn, love people. It must be intentional. In fact, it could be argued that if you don't love people, you do not love God. Discipleship calls us to leave the ninety and nine and to go after the one.

The New Commandment

The next passage is known as the "New Commandment" and is found in John 13:34–35. We see here Jesus saying, "I give you a new commandment: love one another. Just as I have loved you, you must also love one another. By this all people will know that you are My disciples, if you have love for one another." This conversation takes place in the upper room the night that Jesus was delivered over to be crucified. Here, Jesus took the explanation of love one step further. We are to love God. We are to love our neighbor. And, in God's plan, we are to love other brothers and sisters in Christ. Love is the central component in the kingdom of God. God loves us and sent His son. As a result, we can love God. When we love God, we will consequently love our neighbors and we will love other believers. In this passage, Jesus said that all men would know that we are disciples *if* we have love for one another. Put another way, if we don't love our brothers and sisters in Christ, the world has a legitimate right to conclude that we are not followers of Christ.

The Great Example

Let's now look at "the Great Example." After Peter preached on the Day of Pentecost, the Bible says that as many as three thousand people were saved on the first day of the church. So, on the first day of the church age, we see the formation of a "megachurch" that included thousands of followers. This can be seen as a good news/bad news situation. The good news was that there were so many people following Christ. The bad news was that there were suddenly so many people. Can you imagine what the disciples said after Peter preached and the invitation was given and thousands came forward? After baptizing all day and probably the next day, they no doubt convened a meeting and one of the disciples, possibly the skeptical Thomas, said, "What in the world are we going to do now, Peter?" Maybe the conversation went from there to remembering what Jesus told them about loving God, loving people, and loving each other. Maybe one of the others remembered what Jesus said on the mountain about making disciples and how that they (the disciples) were to teach new converts. Maybe one of the others added, "Wait a minute; that's not what He said. He told us to teach them to *observe*. That means we need to teach by example."

Perhaps that is why, when we come to Acts 2:42–47, the early church adopted these habits:

> And they devoted themselves to the apostles' teaching, to fellowship, to the breaking of bread, and to prayers. Then fear came over everyone, and many wonders and signs were being performed through the apostles. Now all the believers were together and had everything in common. So they sold their possessions and property and distributed the proceeds to all, as anyone had a need. And every day they devoted themselves to meeting together in the temple complex, and broke bread from house to house. They ate their food with gladness and simplicity of heart, praising God and having favor with all the people. And every day the Lord added to them those who were being saved.

From this passage alone, we can see up to ten different habits of the early church. They were:

- Studying the apostles' teachings
- Fellowshipping with each other
- Breaking bread together
- Praying

- Finding unity
- Meeting needs
- Worshipping in the temple
- Meeting from "house to house"
- Praising God
- Having favor with all the people

To finish out this passage, as a result of their practicing these habits (disciplined adherence), verse 47 says, "And every day the Lord added to them those who were being saved." The rapid (daily) conversion of the additional believers seems to have been a result of their obedience to the Great Commission. Further, I believe that they met from "house to house" to emphasize the importance of example. The apostle Paul said it this way: "Be imitators of me, as I also am of Christ." In Philippians 4:9, he added, "Do what you have learned and received and heard and seen in me, and the God of peace will be with you." Example is critical to the process of discipleship because Christianity is more caught than taught.

The Great Plan

The next important passage with ecclesiastical implications is Ephesians 4:11–16. I like to call this passage the "Great Plan." The Bible says,

> And He personally gave some to be apostles, some prophets, some evangelists, some pastors and teachers, for the training of the saints in the work of ministry, to build up the body of Christ, until we all reach unity in the faith and in the knowledge of God's Son, growing into a mature man with a stature measured by Christ's fullness. Then we will no longer be little children, tossed by the waves and blown around by every wind of teaching, by human cunning with cleverness in the techniques of deceit. But speaking the truth in love, let us grow in every way into Him who is the head—Christ. From Him the whole body,

fitted and knit together by every supporting ligament, promotes the growth of the body for building
up itself in love by the proper working of each individual part.

Paul wrote Ephesians when he was in prison around AD 62.
In this letter, he clearly identifies the role and function of pastors.
They are to "equip" the saints and the saints are to do the "work
of service" (Eph. 4:12 NASB). The equipping has to do with helping the saints "grow up in all aspects into Him" and to become a
"mature man." Those who practice the spiritual disciplines and
encounter the grace of God will, in turn, be enabled to develop
"Christ likeness." It also involves the body "being fitted together
and held together by what every joint supplies, according to
the proper working of each individual part, [*and that*] causes the
growth of the body" (v. 16 NASB). This involves the disciple discovering and developing his or her gift and developing in the body
(community) to their full potential. (See my previous chapter's
definition on "disciple.")

The Great Ambition

The next verse we want to look at in this section is Colossians
1:28. I call this the "Great Ambition." The apostle Paul writes
these words: "We proclaim Him, admonishing every man and
teaching every man with all wisdom, so that we may present every
man complete in Christ" (NASB). Now this verse is very straight-
forward. If you have ever taken a course on how to study the
Bible, you learn that when the Bible repeats a phrase you need to
pay attention to the repeated phrase. Now look again at the verse
above and see if you can spot the repeated phrase. It is repeated
three times. What is it? The phrase is "every man." The idea here
is that, in our church work, we need to figure out how to minister
and develop every person. From Ephesians chapter four, we know
that we are supposed to "equip the saints." We further learn that
we need to focus on every person in the body. The challenge of

the innovative church is to grow large and small at the same time. If we do not properly focus on the development of the individual, the church will then become impersonal. We can't afford to allow this to happen because the result will be that we cannot transform our culture through transformed lives. We see in this passage that making disciples requires personal attention.

The Great Commission

The last and most famous passage is called the "Great Commission" and is found in Matthew 28:18–20: "Then Jesus came near and said to them, 'All authority has been given to Me in heaven and on earth. Go, therefore, and make disciples of all nations, baptizing them in the name of the Father and of the Son and of the Holy Spirit, teaching them to observe everything I have commanded you. And remember, I am with you always, to the end of the age.'" These words are quite literally the marching orders of the church. This passage contains one command, three participles, and one promise. The command is to "make disciples" (see previous chapter) and the participles that indicate mode are "go" (or more literally "in your going"), "baptizing," and "teaching them to observe." The promise from Jesus is this: "I will be with you." Of course, the promise of the presence and power of Jesus is predicated on obeying the command of making disciples.

From this single passage, we see some very exciting news: every church can enjoy the presence and power of Jesus *if* that church will intentionally, practically, and strategically obey the Great Commission. The central message of the Old Testament is this: "obedience brings blessing and disobedience brings a curse." If we will concentrate on obeying this command, the promise is sure to then follow because God cannot lie. An innovative church is not creating something new, but is rather creating new people, by the grace of God.

This passage is also global in scale because we are to "make disciples of all nations." The only way to reach an exponentially growing world is to implement an exponential strategy. The mission of God is to reach everyone, so the methods we develop need to involve multiplication strategies. That is why church planting is so important. Effective discipleship leads to developing effective leaders for the mission of Christ. The difficult part is for the church to figure out how it will develop disciples who will not only be committed to the person of Christ, but also be committed to the *mission* of Christ. The mission of the church is to reach the world through its disciples.

As a result, there must be an intentional strategy to develop individuals to accomplish the mission of the Master. So let's examine some key dynamics of a church that is effectively generating disciples.

Three Characteristics of a Disciple-Making Church

1. Intentional

Primary Focus: The Great Commandment and the New Commandment

Key Verse: Acts 2:42–47

These passages make it clear that the early church had an unmistakable strategy. That strategy revolved around love—love for God, love for people, and love for believers. This type of love has the ability to crush arguments, confuse enemies, and convince skeptics. In the book of Revelation, we see that the church of Ephesus left its first love and God subsequently gave the church a very specific prescription: "Remember then how far you have fallen; repent, and do the works you did at first. Otherwise, I will come to you and remove your lamp stand from its place—unless you repent" (Rev. 2:5). A church that has lost its love for God won't move forward with love for the lost. The gates of Hades will not be pushed back. Instead, the church will be afflicted with the paralysis of analysis. Maintenance becomes the goal, while a movement is what is needed. When the church does not move forward, it must move backward in retreat. The solution for reaching the world has always been simple, and it is this: people transformed by the grace of God. The church must become intentional in its calling to develop people who genuinely love God, love people, and love believers. This is not a program, this *is* a pursuit. After all, love motivated God to send Jesus in the first place. Love is God's plan for God's people.

2. Individual

Primary Focus: Equipping Christians
Key Verses: Ephesians 4:11–16 and Colossians 1:28
The focus in this series of verses is for pastors to equip the saints for spiritual maturity and for the saints to do the works of service. We are saved to serve. In the Ephesians passage, the emphasis is that every person, "fitted and knit together by every supporting ligament, promotes the growth of the body . . . by the proper working of each individual part." The body of Christ will grow as "each individual part" does its unique and specific function in the body. The converse is true as well: if each part of the body is not functioning properly, then the body will not grow. Church growth is really more of a matter of growing and developing disciples. The body will grow in quantity as it also intentionally develops each individual to reach their full potential in Christ. As the church grows in quantity, it is going to need quality disciples to lead the people in the church by their example. Remember, "Christianity is more caught than taught."

3. Missional

Primary Focus: God's Mandate for World Evangelism
Key Verses: Matthew 2:18–20
This is perhaps the most difficult topic to address because the church often seems to be stuck in what I call a "maintenance mind-set." Pastors are viewed as shepherds who feed and care for difficult sheep instead of a General preparing the good soldiers

for battle. The Great Commission makes it clear that we are to make disciples "of all nations." Yet, every year we seem to get further and further behind in this calling. Why would God give us a mandate that seems so impossible to accomplish? The answer is: He didn't. It is possible to reach the world with the gospel if we understand that the full development of every person is critical to reaching the world. As the person grows in Christlikeness and maturity, we intentionally create opportunities for them to engage directly in the mission of the Master. We cannot reach the world if we do not equip the saints to reach their full potential.

Discipleship Action Points

Based upon these principles, here is my definition of discipleship: *Discipleship is the process of guiding individual disciples to grow in spiritual maturity and to discover and use their gifts, talents, and abilities in fulfillment of Christ's mission.* Now let's examine some "action points" regarding discipleship.

Make Disciples

The church must come to grips with the clear call of the Great Commission to "make disciples." The local church is the expression of the kingdom of God, and the kingdom is the expression of the mission of God, and the mission springs from the heart of God. In order to accomplish the mission, the church must develop disciples to their full potential. The way to grow the body is to grow the individual. The way to reach the world is to develop disciples to their full potential. The question for each and every local church is: "How do we accomplish this?"

The answer of how to properly make a disciple is tied to the definition of what a disciple looks like. This is my definition of a disciple, based upon the principles that Jesus gave: *A disciple is a person who has trusted Christ for salvation and has surrendered completely to Him. He or she is committed to practicing the spiritual disciplines in community and developing to their full potential for Christ and His mission.*

Assimilation

A local church must intentionally set about to create that type of follower of Christ. To make a disciple you must first win the person to Christ; therefore the local church must discover and develop evangelistic approaches that are effective in leading people to salvation. The next thing a disciple needs is the ability to become connected to the local church. This means that the local church needs to seriously think through how to connect a disciple to groups and ministries within the local church. The word *assimilation* is used here. The Great Commission emphasizes the aspect of "teaching them to observe" so the growing disciple needs good examples. Therefore, the church needs to have a group ministry that is intentional and developmental. This group ministry can be a medium-sized group or even a small group wherein individuals can be challenged to grow through imitation.

Ministry Progression

As the disciple grows in Christlikeness, the church needs to help that person discover his/her gifts and abilities for the kingdom. And so the church needs to help the disciple learn to serve. Currently the "program-driven church" has many entry level places for disciples to serve, but the church must be careful to maintain a priority on disciple-making ministries. Specifically a local church needs to help disciples with leadership potential become apprentices in Great Commission ministries by mentoring those disciples to the point where they become leaders in the multiplication ministries of the church. Finally, there are a percentage of disciples, when they are fully developed, who need to be involved in the planting and starting of new churches. Again, the world is rapidly growing and we must employ exponential strategies in order to take the gospel to new generations of people.

The disciples who develop to this point have learned to conduct pastoral ministry inside their local church and are then ready to advance the kingdom and mission of God by either being a part of a new church-plant project or in actually leading the plant.

Conclusion

Can you imagine what would happen if every church planted one additional church? There are approximately 330,000 churches in America today. If every church planted a church, we would have 660,000 churches! The impact of such an action would change our world. If our nation experienced this type of church growth, reaching the world with the gospel would not be a distant dream; it would become a reality. But please understand this: the starting point is in winning the people in your town to Christ, teaching them to reach their full potential, and eventually sending them into other parts of the world. The formula is: **Win. Grow. Send.** In this formula, we see that discipleship and church planting are intrinsically linked because when a disciple "has been fully trained, he will be like his teacher."[3] God sent Jesus to this world to redeem it and now Jesus calls us to make disciples. The process of making disciples is called discipleship and it looks like this: *Discipleship is the process of guiding individual disciples to grow in spiritual maturity and to discover and use their gifts, talents, and abilities in fulfillment of Christ's mission.*

My hope and prayer is that, as you read this book, you will accept the challenge to become a disciple-making church. If you become a disciple maker or if your church becomes a disciple-making church, you will then qualify to receive the promise of the Great Commission, which is the presence and power of Jesus.

Notes

1. *Fox's Book of Martyrs* (Grand Rapids, MI: Zondervan, 1978).
2. http://biblecommenters.com/matthew/16-18.html.
3. Source unknown.

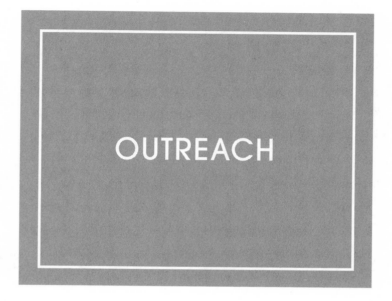

OUTREACH

CHAPTER 8

Outreach: Back to Basics in Strategic Planning

by David Wheeler

After many years of consulting with hundreds of congregations across the country, I became frustrated with the lack of biblical multiplication resulting in new disciples and baptisms. While the churches I have studied largely focused on new programs or other agendas, they continued to see declining numbers. The obvious question remained: "Where is the natural multiplication and growth as the living body of Christ?"

The "Back to Basics" process is not merely another emphasis or program. On the contrary, it is a step-by-step guide that points a person or congregation back to the foundational call of where one should be in relation to Scripture, as lived out in practical daily ministry. In a nutshell, the process strives to reestablish, without apology or compromise, evangelism as the key holistic priority of the church.

How Does "Back to Basics" Work?

There are five basic concerns that are addressed in the "Back to Basics" process. Keep in mind that each of the areas we discuss is essential in leading one's congregation to adopt a biblical understanding of how they should function as a community seeking to impact the world for Christ.

At some points there are actual structural changes that are suggested for the church in order to become more strategic and focused on multiplication. At other points, like the emphasis on recovering the church and evangelism, it is a simple matter of leadership reestablishing the biblical definition and model by way of the pulpit and small groups.

In each case I believe the church must examine itself from a biblical perspective and be bold in making proper adjustments to enhance effectiveness. The process is enumerated as follows:

1. Back to Basics in Recovering the Biblical Church

The first major challenge is defining the church as an organism, rather than a mere organization. Think about it: how does our culture normally explain the idea of church? The usual response defines church as a location, building, something you do, or somewhere to go. Sadly, all of these usual explanations see church as an organization, not as an organism.

In fact, even with the establishment of the new covenant, we practice church in more of an Old Testament model than a New Testament expression. We typically treat church as a temple in which we worship, not as a body of believers. Much like the Pharisees, we also tend to deify our legalisms and preferences, even if it is driving people away from Christ, rather than attracting people to Him. The sad part is that God has much more for the church to experience, rather than simply hanging grace and mercy from an Old Testament model. Why should God bless us when we refuse to become what He has called us to live out?

Even the phrase we hear so much in prayer—"thank You God for bringing us to Your house today"—isn't really proper New Testament ecclesiology. The truth is that in the New Covenant, God abides in the hearts of men, not brick and mortar. A deeper understanding of this will radically change a person and innovate how they go about living out their faith and doing outreach in daily life.

Furthermore, if we view church as existing in a separate location from which we live, then it becomes easy to ignore ethical mandates and especially Great Commission responsibilities relating to outreach. However, if we genuinely understand that we are the church in flesh, our neighborhoods and workplaces become mission fields in which we share Christ in both words and behavior. In addition, if a congregation is defined as primarily an organization, it will usually become a church that goes from one event/ program to another in evangelism, rather than developing a holistic biblical strategy centered on the principles of the harvest.

Ultimately an organizational mind-set breeds a mentality of addition over biblical multiplication. If this is not recognized and corrected, the driving force of ministry becomes a stressful numbers game that is more interested in the "bottom line" than it is in creating disciples. In turn, this "bottom line" mentality can easily become a source of arrogance and bragging rights that has little to do with expanding the kingdom and creating a movement of God, and much more to do with building up the ego and reputation of the organization leader.

If this assertion were not true, why is it so difficult to get church leaders to surrender members to plant new congregations? Believe it or not, much of this mentality goes back to an unbiblical model of church and how it is to be defined. In reality, the "bottom line" must always be driven by the desire to multiply at every level of ministry and to give it away to the glory of Christ, not man. By nature, organizations find it almost impossible to multiply. On the other hand, just as our cells naturally multiply as living organisms, the same must be true in how we interpret the nature of church to our congregations. This is imperative to building a Great Commission mentality and innovating the concepts of outreach among believers. As L. E. Boyston once said, "As it relates to the church, organization should be a verb, not a noun . . . when organization becomes a noun, church has changed its essential nature."[1]

2. Back to Basics in Recovering Biblical Evangelism

Evangelism is typically defined in narrow terms relating to the initial encounter with the gospel. In fact, when approached, people usually define evangelism in negative expressions that conjure up feelings of deep fear and oppression. For the most part evangelism is totally misunderstood as it relates to the ministry of the church. For instance, some people see evangelism as a spiritual gift only designed for the few unlucky warriors. On the contrary, evangelism is not a spiritual gift! The word is actually a noun (*euaggelion*), not a verb (*euaggelidzo*). In other words, by its very nature one has to define evangelism by what it is, not by what it does.

So what is it? By definition, evangelism means "good news." Evangelism is the message! Therefore it is not reserved for the chosen few, rather it is the imperative and task of the whole church as an organism (see Acts 1:8 "be My witnesses").

I recently spoke with a vice president of a major Christian institution in the Midwest. He strongly suggested that we shouldn't use the word *evangelism* in reference to his students, because to them, evangelism was a negative term and carried frightful recollections. Wow! When did evangelicals lose their passion for evangelism?

Another misunderstanding is that evangelism is only one of several tasks that the church must complete. Narrowly understood, that could be a true statement. However, when evangelism is properly and intricately understood in terms of worship, discipleship, prayer, missions, fellowship, and ministry, it is no longer defined in such narrow expressions. For instance, proper discipleship is never complete until the person being discipled multiplies their witness consistently into those who do not know Christ.

Furthermore, contrary to what many people assume, the word *missions* is not interchangeable with the word *evangelism* either. By nature missions is the process of contextualizing the gospel message into culture. On the other hand, evangelism *is* the message! Thus, it is entirely possible for a person to evoke the process of evangelism without actually doing missions. However, it is impossible to do real missions without doing evangelism.

The usual result of improperly defining evangelism and missions is that the church will spend their energies and resources obsessing over the contextual tools like demographic studies, research, mapping, etc., without actually exalting the message and seeing people come to Christ. It is not that these contextual studies are not helpful or even important; rather it is that Jesus instructed the church in John 12:32, "If I am lifted up . . . I will draw all people to Myself."

Again, a proper understanding of evangelism as the message of Christ, demands that the church prioritize the gospel itself rather than glorifying the tools of expressing that same gospel. To do any different would be like a fisherman who always brags about his fish-finding tools, but never actually catches any fish. The bottom line is that the church is called to be "fishers of men" (Mark 1:17 NASB), not "finders of men." As fishermen, the priority is always to catch fish.

Evangelism is usually thought of in the narrowest of terms as simply sharing the right information. However, while it is important to verify the proper information, that is only half of the message and ignores consideration of the relational and social expressions. In other words, it is impossible to divorce Jesus' message from the Person He represented. Therefore, true evangelism must always embrace the whole being in both words and deeds. Anything less will normally result in dry and lifeless orthodoxy or liberalism.

The challenge is that most church leaders are unwilling to admit that evangelism should be the main priority of the body.

Could it be that they are simply intimidated by the task, or maybe they do not understand the holistic connection of evangelism with every other responsibility of the church? The problem is that we tend to ignore those things for which we do not attach intentionality. Quite simply, it is easier and less intimidating to maintain the organizational assignments of the church than it is to embrace the call of Christ who Himself "came to seek and to save those who are lost" (Luke 19:10).

Most people never consider that the Bible is primarily a book about evangelism. You may be asking how this can be. Let's think about it: if you take the message of redemption out of Scripture, what is left? A proper understanding of evangelism must include both the act of sharing redemption, as well as being the message itself. Therefore, assuming that Jesus' main purpose in coming to the world was to provide redemption, is it not logical to assume that His church should also prioritize the sharing of that same redemptive message?

As long as Satan is allowed to minimize evangelism in the eyes of the body and to divorce it from the call of the church, the Great Commission will continue to suffer. For the sake of biblical multiplication, it is imperative that the church understands evangelism in the broadest sense. Evangelism, properly understood, must be reestablished as the main purpose of the church, not merely one of numerous functions.

3. Back to Basics through a Mentoring/ Accountability Process

The heart and soul of this approach is defined through the mentoring process. It is here that congregations and their leaders will be held accountable on an individual basis to remain true to the biblical commitments relating to the harvest.

The mentoring aspect of "Back to Basics" was developed after observing numerous church leaders (pastors and staff) over the course of several years. After a period of time in ministry, many of these leaders slowly begin to abandon their passionate calls to transform lives in order to simply maintain the organizational structures of the church.

Unfortunately committee meetings and putting out fires replace evangelism, building relationships, and multiplying disciples. As discussed earlier, in way too many cases the goal of ministry becomes a numbers game that has little to do with kingdom growth and more to do with self-exaltation and protecting one's job.

The sad part is that over time many of these leaders acknowledged their compromise but felt trapped in the unbiblical roles and expectations they were given. As stress and lack of fulfillment grows, so does the exodus of numerous men and women from ministry. As I have been told by hundreds of pastors and staff leaders over the last several years: "All I want to do in ministry is be a conduit of Christ, in order to change lives." This is what "Back to Basics" is all about.

The mentoring/accountability process is designed to be simple yet profound, straight to the point, and easy to accommodate in a busy schedule. The four accountability points of this approach are designed to help the participants redevelop life habits resulting in a mentality of genuine biblical multiplication.

Here is how it works. First, each participant must have two other accountability partners with the commitment to set aside a brief time on a weekly basis to answer four simple questions. They do not have to meet in person, as a weekly phone call at a designated time is acceptable.

Keep in mind that the four commitment statements are designed to reflect the harvest principles to be discussed in the next section of Back to Basics. That is to plow through prayer, plant the gospel seed, then comes the harvest! The four accountability points are as follows:

1. Commit to having a daily quiet time (not sermon preparation) and, as part of this, keeping a list of unsaved people and pray for them daily (*plowing*).

2. Commit to sharing your faith with at least one person each week (outside of the church setting) with the aim, as the Holy Spirit leads, to draw the net (*planting and harvesting*).

3. Commit to doing at least one significant "servanthood evangelism" activity per month in your community (*planting and sometimes harvesting*).

4. Commit to multiplying yourself by mentoring at least one person in your sphere of influence per year, in order to adopt these life principles.

You may be wondering about how and why these particular points were adopted. The reason is, for the sake of simplicity, each point grew out of honest observations, personal experiences, and numerous discussions with church leaders over the last decade. For instance, it is well known that many church leaders struggle to have a daily quiet time that is not attached to sermon preparation or hindered by organizational expectations. Sadly, most churches will admit that they rarely, if ever, pray for the unsaved.

Furthermore, statistics reveal that a large number of church leaders rarely share their faith outside of the church setting. Please understand that we are not talking about simply inviting people to church. On the contrary, the real issue is whether church leaders and congregations are actually sharing their faith on a regular basis, therefore planting sufficient seeds for a plentiful harvest.

As for "servanthood evangelism" activities, this aspect is designed to mobilize the church body into their own neighborhoods. (See the next chapter for outreach ideas.) After hundreds of conversations with church leaders and congregations, it is shocking to discover that most people do not know their neighbors. How can the church have a multiplication movement if God's people do not feel any responsibility to evangelize the mission field outside their front doors?

Unfortunately, because of a prevailing organizational church mentality, we seem to be content to drive out of our "Jerusalem" to practice church busyness without ever being the church where we live. In addition, it has been my observation that the majority of pastors I speak with, if they are honest, usually fall into this category. If this is true, then it is easy to understand why congregations have lost their evangelistic zeal. After all, as the congregational leader, one can realistically expect to influence and guide people only as far as he is right now. That is, we generally replicate what we value and practice.

The final aspect of the process is designed to return the church to the business of biblical discipleship. It has been well stated that the aim of evangelism must always go beyond the initial salvation decision. Again, when properly understood, the goal of biblical evangelism must always be the multiplication of genuine disciples/ worshipers.

One person per year may sound miniscule, and it is. Nevertheless, if followed correctly, it should begin a multiplication process as the ones being discipled are expected to return to the basics and mentor others to do the same in the following years. The bottom line is unless we internalize these harvest principles as an expression of our individual core value of multiplication, it is unrealistic to expect a radical change in the direction and growth of the church.

4. Back to Basics through Establishing a Strategic Process

Understanding the Essential Harvest Principles

After one truly understands the key issues related to properly defining the church, evangelism, as well as the mentoring process aimed at changing unfruitful habits, the next step is to initiate a strategic plan. The background for this approach is found in Scripture passages such as Psalm 126:5–6 and John 4:35–38, where the principles of the harvest are discussed. For the sake of explanation, the biblical principles highlighted in these passages help to reengage the church in the process of plowing through prayer, planting the gospel seed, and then the harvest will naturally come.

The truth is, regardless of the church growth materials one reads, the biblical principles are always the same. Properly understood, the harvest is a natural outcome that can only be halted when the principles are ignored. In other words, the only way to kill the harvest is to not plow and plant. So, before discussing strategic structures and approaches to innovate the church in the area of outreach, there must be a clear understanding of how the harvest works. Unfortunately this is where most churches stray off course.

While most church leaders are looking for a quick fix that will immediately result in enormous growth, the wise thing is to take an inventory of the church's current approaches in light of principles leading to the harvest. For instance, does your church have an ongoing prayer ministry that regularly encourages the whole congregation to pray for the unsaved? Based upon the mentoring principles explained earlier, is the congregation encouraged to keep a list of unsaved acquaintances and pray for them daily? If not, why? Keep in mind that if the plowing is ignored, the seed may never sink into the soil.

How is your congregation mobilized to plant the gospel seed? Considering that most people rarely engage another person in a gospel conversation or service activity, there is little doubt why the harvest is so lean and baptisms are declining. Just like a farmer, the church must generously plant the gospel seed if a harvest is to be expected. After all, the harvest is God's business, the call of the church is to faithfully plow and plant. If ignored, the church cannot grow and be healthy.

A Suggested Strategic Structure

In addition to the essential principles of the harvest, there is a suggested structure of how to become a people that reflect these principles in every area of congregational expressions. In order to understand what makes this approach different, pay attention to the following comparisons.

Traditionally, most congregations design their strategy around a basic mission statement that is lived out through five purposes of the church. They are: worship, evangelism, fellowship, ministry, and discipleship (see diagram #1).

DIAGRAM #1
"Traditional" Model

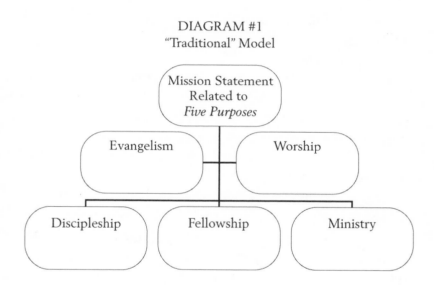

The problem with this structure is that it treats evangelism as only one of five expressions of the church. Again, properly understood, evangelism is not a mere compartment of God's strategy relating to the church, rather it is the engine that drives intentionality and direction for every aspect and outcome of the congregation. It is a major mistake to assume that evangelism is being addressed just because it is mentioned. For example, from personal experience, many congregations appear to be happy by fulfilling four of the five responsibilities mentioned above. Based on the latest baptismal trends in the Southern Baptist Convention, obviously evangelism is the one responsibility that is ignored.

This is called the Eighty Percent Principle. This occurs when a church seems content to attempt fulfilling 80 percent of their basic responsibilities without multiplying through evangelism. The truth is, if churches were genuinely fulfilling the 80 percent, to some degree, evangelism would be a natural by-product. Unfortunately this is the usual result when the church is seen as an organization, and evangelism is narrowly defined and not given proper biblical interpretation. Evangelism must never be communicated as a mere suggestion or displaced among numerous responsibilities; on the contrary, it is a command from Christ Himself (see Acts 1:8: "be My witnesses").

Conversely, in "Back to Basics," the strategic structure reorganizes the responsibilities to reflect an evangelistic priority. To begin with, there is a mission statement that intentionally points to the Great Commission and directs people back to the cross of Christ. This is rarely achieved, especially as it relates to the cross. A mission statement should always reflect God's priorities and say more about Him than us! Again, as Jesus said, "If I am lifted up . . . I will draw all people to Myself" (John 12:32).

The next level falls directly under the Mission Statement. For lack of a better title, it is referred to as the "Harvest Council." Rather than diffusing evangelism out as one of five responsibilities, it is moved up and incorporated into the harvest council. (See diagram #2 on the next page.)

Along with the church staff, the council has representatives from each of the other five functions (since evangelism is elevated up under the umbrella of the harvest council, prayer replaces evangelism and the other functions remain the same). In essence, the council acts as a filter for strategic planning, budgeting, calendaring, etc., in order to assure evangelistic intentionality is part of every aspect of congregational life.

It works something like this. Normally a church will plan numerous fellowship activities in an average church year. These activities usually occur without any question as to evangelistic intentionality or purpose. Under this approach, if a church intends

DIAGRAM # 2
"Back to Basics" Model

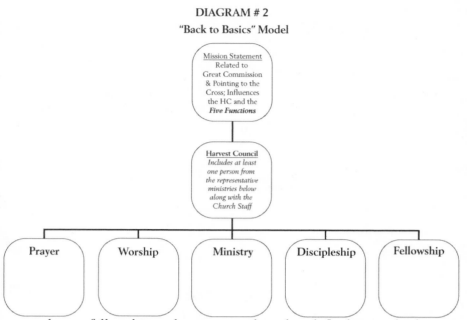

to have a fellowship and wants to utilize church facilities or budget funds, there must be a strategic drive to include the unsaved into the activities. Think about it, when was the last time you attended a fellowship at church where a significant number of unsaved people were in attendance? Without a structure to create intentionality, unfortunately evangelism is usually an afterthought.

This must also be true as the church intentionally includes intercession for the unsaved into their prayer ministries; or discipleship ministries that intentionally seek to create believers who will multiply their witness; or an approach to worship that celebrates redemption and prioritizes evangelism; or ministries that are not merely for the redeemed inside the church walls, but are designed with real evangelism as the driving force. As Archbishop William Temple once said, "The church is the only cooperative society in the world that exists for the benefit of its nonmembers!"[2]

Beware the naysayers who complain by saying, "This is unbalanced because evangelism cannot be the main priority." Again, when evangelism is properly understood as an intricate part and driving force of each of the five functions, it is then that Christians truly become "fishers of men." The church should not apologize because it is driven by the imperative to reach the unsaved.

Remember, under a holistic/biblical view of evangelism, it does not stop at the moment of decision. In fact, evangelism is never complete until the person is incarnationally driven to multiply their witness experientially and verbally with the unsaved as a part of a normal daily life. When this occurs, genuine disciples are created.

Along with a strong mission statement, the harvest council reflects the heartbeat of the congregation and acts as a plumb line of accountability to make sure that the church does not lose sight of its Great Commission goal. Remember, it is all about intentionality and biblical multiplication.

5. Back to Basics through Biblical Multiplication

The ultimate outcome of this process is to elevate biblical multiplication of congregations and disciples as a personal core value of why the church exists. According to most reports concerning the church, this is obviously a struggling concept.

Consider for a moment that according to some of the most recent data from the North American Mission Board of the Southern Baptist Convention, only 4.8 percent of churches sponsored a church-type mission in 2006. Furthermore, according to additional studies only 15.3 percent of Southern Baptist pastors stated that they participated at any level in a church planting venture during the same period.

It wasn't too many years ago that Southern Baptists understood their Great Commission responsibility and propagated a favorable mentality toward church planting. Back in the 1940s and 1950s, there were major movements like the Western and Pioneer Advance, the Five Year Crusade for Christ, Four Year Conquest for Christ, and the Thirty-Thousand Movement/Baptist Jubilee Advance. While contextualization into culture was not a major priority during these movements, the raw numbers will support the fact that average Southern Baptists were exposed to church planting and could see multiplication at work.

Unfortunately this is no longer true regardless of denominational affiliation. Sadly, as a professor at a Christian university, it is rare to meet seminary or college students who have been previously exposed to church planting at any level before coming to school.

The goal of this area of "Back to Basics" is to build upon the foundation that has been laid in the previous four sections. After all, biblical multiplication should be the natural outcome of a proper definition relating to the church and evangelism. In addition, both the mentoring process and the strategic structure should further support a multiplication mind-set. Ultimately, just as multiplication illuminates from the heart of God, it must also shine brightly through the organisms that make up His church.

This is the guiding value and passion of "Back to Basics." For more information relating to church planting and multiplication, please refer to chapter 11, written by Dr. Dave Earley.

Where do we go from here?

It is imperative to remember that in order to truly innovate outreach in the life of the local church, there must be a proper understanding of strategic planning. It begins with a biblical definition of "church." If it is organic in nature, it will naturally emanate life and multiply as it grows. This is why we call it a body.

There must also be a holistic understanding of evangelism as it relates to every function of the church. Properly defined, do not hesitate to reestablish evangelism as both the purpose and priority of your congregation.

Finally, utilize the mentoring process with church leaders and consider reestablishing a strategic structure similar to the one outlined in section 4 of this chapter. Most of all, do not forget the harvest principles. They may appear to be simplistic and old-fashioned. Nevertheless, the principles are biblically sound and must never be ignored. Sometimes, in order to innovate, it first requires going "Back to Basics."

Notes

1. Gary Bulley, "What Is Church" in *Introduction to Church Planting* (North American Mission Board, 2000).

2. *The Evangelism Planner* (North American Mission Board, 2004).

CHAPTER 9

Innovate Outreach: Back to Basics in Strategic Harvesting

by David Wheeler

After establishing a strategic process and plan for multiplication and congregational growth, it is always important to
secure the methodologies that will assist in bringing the vision
to fruition. These methodologies and related activities are important, but must never operate outside of the ongoing biblical principles that were discussed in the previous chapter. To do so will
seriously hinder the creation of an ongoing multiplication movement that exalts Christ and fulfills His purpose to "seek and save
those who are lost" (Luke 19:10).

While it is impossible to deal with every approach to Innovate
Outreach, the following suggestions will assist in the challenge.
The goal is not to encourage the total abandonment of all current
activities, but to insert intentionality into every aspect of how the
church is manifested and mobilized into the community. The three
strategic areas to be discussed relate to evangelistic preaching,

building intentional relationships, and harvesting through evangelistic events/presentations.

Drawing the Net through Evangelistic Preaching

Developing a Strategic Plan for Evangelistic Preaching

While it is always important to plan the subject matter and direction of a sermon series, this must never be the end. On the contrary, in a day when it is normal to preach a cute series with psychological suggestions pertaining to "ten ways" to change a lightbulb, there must be a biblical foundation that is grounded in a strategic process seeking to change lives. In other words, biblical communicators must understand that their job is not to simply entertain or keep people coming back. The ultimate goal is to set the vision based upon God's leadership and utilize the pulpit to disciple the congregation in the direction of the outreach vision.

For instance, if a pastor was going to utilize the information gained in the previous chapter relating to the "Back to Basics" strategic planning process, he would need to aim his preaching in a desired direction to mobilize the congregation into the harvest fields. To do this, it would require the willingness to regularly ask for some form of commitment. Unfortunately much of the preaching today does not ask for a response, nor does it attempt to create a cohesive vision.

So, how should this planning materialize? Let's say you want to mobilize the church for the sake of evangelism. Again, based upon the previous chapter, it would be wise if you wanted to communicate the "Back to Basics" process, to first begin by preaching a series on "Recovering the Biblical Church." The initial series would obviously emphasize the imperative of the church before becoming an organism and could be drawn from the life of Christ in the Gospels. This would include basic outreach assignments aimed at reaching into a person's incarnational (or living) sphere where they live, work, and play.

The next series might include an emphasis on "Recovering Biblical Evangelism." This could be taken from several chapters in Acts and would include a continued emphasis on the church as an organism that is being mobilized into the world. This could also include a study into the individual call of evangelism by challenging the notion that it is a spiritual gift only reserved for the few. The aim is to reconnect the congregation with evangelism as it relates to every ministry of the church.

After walking through the process of recovering the biblical church and evangelism, one could utilize the "Back to Basics" mentoring process as another sermon series. This could be accomplished by preaching a sermon each week related to one of the basic commitments in the mentoring process. This could result in the congregation being challenged to adopt the mentoring process as part of their weekly discipleship.

From this point the next progression of "Back to Basics" would be an investigation into changing the structure of how your church operates. You could build upon previous sermons aimed at bringing the church to this point of decision. Remember, the pulpit should always have a strong component that aims to disciple the congregation in the direction of the evangelistic vision. That is, to mobilize the congregation into action that results in natural multiplication of disciples and congregations.

The emphasis of the previous paragraphs is not to sell you on the "Back to Basics" process. On the contrary, it merely serves as an example of how a pastor could move his congregation in a desired direction over several months by utilizing the pulpit to establish a heartbeat for evangelism. Each new sermon series builds upon previous strategic challenges and becomes a catalyst to move the congregation in the direction of the evangelistic vision. Keep in mind that this is an intentional process that emphasizes consistently proclaiming the principles of the harvest in front of the congregation.

In the end, aimless ramblings and clever sermons will not result in a strategic process of evangelism if they are not tied to the overall vision and direction of the congregation. A wise pastor realizes that evangelism is a harvesting process that requires strategic thinking and planning to move the congregation in a desired direction. He is not simply looking for another stand-alone sermon series. Rather he prayerfully sees the end from the beginning and is always moving the congregation toward the evangelistic vision.

Giving an Effective Evangelistic Invitation

Believe it or not, there are numerous pastors today who believe that altar calls are no longer necessary. If this is true, exactly how is the preacher to treat the end of a service? Unfortunately in many cases the invitation is being conveniently ignored. At the very least, the invitation is not being handled in an effective manner. Further, in a growing number of congregations, contemporary pastors are utilizing commitment cards in the pew and follow-up rooms as significant opportunities to deal with all kinds of decisions. It is nothing new; everyone (including church members) simply fills out a commitment card each service and places it in the offering plate or turns it in as they leave the building. The follow-up rooms are simply places for "seekers" to gather with the church staff in order to build relationships and to ask spiritual questions in a smaller and less intimidating setting. In each case, personal discipleship/evangelism is the key to reaping a future harvest.

As noted, the surprising trend in some circles is not to offer an invitation at all, at least not after every sermon. While a pastor may not choose to give an invitation in every instance, to have a policy of never extending the opportunity for people to respond is akin to going fishing without a hook. In this case, don't be shocked if you never catch any fish.

The truth is, based upon the ministries of Jesus, Paul, Peter, and numerous others in the Bible, it is imperative that God's man should not ignore the opportunity to allow for an evangelistic response. While it should never be manipulative or coercive, it should always be intentional and well prepared.

After all, as John 6:44 tells us: "No one can come to Me unless the Father who sent Me draws him." Thus, a proper invitation is simply the process of the Father utilizing faithful men to be His messengers of hope as He draws the net. Yet, how will they respond if the invitation is never given?

To some, this is a matter of God's sovereignty. In these cases, the invitation is somehow a theological violation of personal convictions. Granted, there must always be a strong sense of integrity attached to the invitation, but the proposition should not be avoided because of irrational fears that someone might respond outside of God's calling.

With this in mind, it may be timely to recall the previous chapter in reference to the principles of the harvest. While the church is called to plow and plant, the harvesting is always the business of God. Man does not create the harvest, but if the fields are, as Jesus states in John 4:35 (NASB), "white for harvest," through the invitation the preacher uniquely becomes a partner in the harvest with Christ.

In addition to the above suggestions, as "fishers of men," a wise pastor should also spend significant time planning for the invitation just as he does working through the biblical passage. The invitation should never appear as an appendage that is merely tacked onto the end of the message. On the contrary, the invitation should flow smoothly from the message and must always illicit some type of response.

Obviously calling for people to respond to Christ through salvation should be the primary concern. However, calling people for prayer, recommitment, church membership, baptism, and surrendering to full-time ministry are also valid appeals to be used during the invitation. Most of this can be accomplished by utilizing the invitation in a come-forward style. It can also be done in less invasive ways like the commitment cards or follow-up rooms mentioned earlier. The key is to plan your follow-up as you prepare for the invitation.

The bottom line is that the invitation is an important and essential part of building an evangelistic pulpit and an effective church ministry. The wise pastor must never be afraid to ask for a response to the message of the gospel. After all, as it states in Hebrews 4:12, "The word of God is living and powerful" (NKJV). Thus, by its very nature, when the Word of God is proclaimed, it stirs the hearts of men to action and repentance. The invitation, regardless of the mode, is a dynamic way of allowing people the opportunity to express commitment and surrender to Christ as Lord.

Drawing the Net through "Intentional" Relationships

Over the years one of the raging battles in conservative evangelical circles has been the constant tension in evangelism between building relationships (incarnational) and simply sharing the message (informational). The perception has been that liberals served people's needs without ever sharing the message. On the contrary, in many cases the conservatives would aggressively share the message without ever considering the needs of the recipients.

The truth is, evangelism is not an either/or proposition, rather it requires both dimensions to be effective. It is a serious mistake to ignore either approach. Think about it: to meet people's incarnational needs without sharing the gospel message will often lead to heresy. At the same time, to simply share the informational requirements of the gospel without being concerned with the incarnational components relating to people's needs will often lead to hypocrisy. In short, it is impossible to divorce the message of Jesus from the man He represented.

With this in mind, the following relational approaches are meant to compliment the informational gospel and to work in conjunction with the Holy Spirit to create intentional evangelistic opportunities. They are:

Servanthood Evangelism

Servanthood evangelism is a combination of simple acts of kindness and intentional personal evangelism. The concept is as old as the New Testament. Like many profound truths, this one is so simple it is easily missed: get a group of believers, preferably at a local church, and begin practicing simple acts of kindness with an intentional aim toward evangelism. In many cases, such acts of kindness open the door for the greatest act of kindness a Christian can give: the gospel.

Understand what kindness means. It does not mean telling people what they want to hear so they will feel good about themselves. Servanthood evangelism involves more than mere acts of kindness. There are valuable ministries, such as taking a loaf of bread to newcomers, and others, which are helpful, but they are not explicitly evangelistic. Servanthood evangelism is intentionally evangelistic, though by no means does it seek to coerce in a negative sense.

When carrying out an act of kindness, the witness says, "I am doing this to show the love of Jesus in a practical way." Then, as the Holy Spirit opens the door, usually through the individual responding, the one performing the act of servanthood has a captive audience and proceeds to share their conversion testimony coupled with the gospel presentation.[1]

Projects like giving out water bottles or cold sodas at summer community festivals or popsicles in the park, washing someone's car without charge, or giving out lightbulbs door to door are effective evangelistic tools. But they represent the surface level of servanthood evangelism. Keep in mind that servanthood is not a program; rather it is a heart response by a committed believer. Thus, it cannot become an assignment or an evangelistic methodology; it must become part of the congregational DNA.

Three Servanthood Evangelism Projects that Work

1. Gas "buy-down." Secure a local gas station and buy-down every gallon of gas that is sold from 11:00 a.m. to

1:00 p.m. by twenty-five cents per gallon, up to twenty
gallons per car. If the gas is $3.00 per gallon, it would be
sold for $2.75 per gallon and the church will make up the
difference. Church members will pump the gas and wash
windshields.

2. Adopt local public schools. Take fresh donuts to the
    teacher's lounge each week. Volunteer to take up tickets
    for sporting events or feed the teachers for free on
    in-service days.

3. Use "intentional connection cards." The cards can say
    something as simple as, "We just want you to know
    that we care." On the back might be a small map to
    the church and other pertinent information. The cards
    are good for any servant evangelism activity, but when
    utilized by Christians—in cases like anonymously paying
    someone's bill in a restaurant, or paying for the drive-
    through meal of the passengers behind you—it is an
    effective way to plant seeds.

Go to www.innovatechurch.us under "outreach" for more
information and unique ideas on servanthood evangelism. Also go
to www.servantevangelism.com.

Ministry Evangelism

Ministry evangelism and servanthood evangelism are similar in
many ways. Both approaches seek to meet people's needs in order
to intentionally open the doors for the gospel message. However,
the main difference rests in the issue of personal versus corporate
outreach. In other words, the ultimate aim of servanthood evangelism is to mobilize individual Christians to incarnationally engage
their communities both inside and outside of the corporate setting
of the church. Servanthood evangelism can be done through large
corporate events, but this is not the ultimate goal.

Conversely, ministry evangelism usually grows out of the
local church as individual's work together to meet corporate

needs. For instance, feeding centers, crisis pregnancy centers, after-school tutoring, disaster relief, and English as a second language ministries are all corporately driven out of the larger church body and usually through the church facilities. These types of ministries are extremely evangelistic and allow church members to team together to meet needs and share Christ in a more controlled setting.

Other approaches may include disabilities awareness, substance abuse, migrant workers, and medical/dental ministries. In addition, it can also include specialized ministries like resort and leisure ministries, truck-stop ministries, and prison outreaches.

For more information on these and other ministry opportunities, go to www.namb.net and do a search for "Ministry/Servant Evangelism."

Community Groups

Community groups are a major outreach tool at Thomas Road Baptist Church in Lynchburg, Virginia. The groups are designed to get unchurched and/or de-churched people in the church buildings for the purpose of meeting their needs and giving the gospel a chance to be heard by these people who need it most. The groups may offer numerous types of educational and practical opportunities, such as assorted kinds of crafts, hunting and fishing, car repair and restoration, preparing tax returns, gourmet cooking, etc. The approach is a unique combination of both servanthood evangelism and ministry evangelism. While it is done on the church property, this effort requires incarnational intervention through the simple stair-step process of:

- Win the person to yourself
- Win the person to the church
- Win the person to Christ

In addition, church members are encouraged to "pray" for the participants; "care" for the participants; then seek to "share" with the unsaved participants. The groups meet on the church property for eight weeks, three times a year with promotion and recruiting in the off months. They meet for one hour on Wednesday evenings, which includes a brief devotional (usually from *Our Daily Bread*).

As time goes by, the aim is to look for connection points during the weeks and eventually invite people to come for Sunday services. The church members are prayerfully "intentional," but very careful not to rush the process.

For more information concerning the community groups, go to www.trbc.org or to www.innovatechurch.us under "outreach."

The SHOT Principle

The SHOT Principle (somewhere, help, our place, their place) was developed for the book *Friends Forever*. The approach is very simple, yet tremendously effective. Each letter of the acrostic stands for a different relational approach to engaging an unsaved person over an extended period (preferably six weeks or less).

The initial aim is to invite an unsaved neighbor or friend to go *somewhere* with you. It could be a ball game, dinner, etc. Hopefully, this will begin the relational dialogue. The next step is to ask this person to assist in a "*help* ministry" project, such as painting an elderly person's home, etc. Believe it or not, most unsaved people are perfectly willing to assist in these types of projects. This will also further the relational dialogue.

The next step is to invite the person or family to your (our) place for a meal and more relationship building. After establishing trust, the final step is to go to *their* place. If one's testimony and personal faith have not already been shared through previous encounters, assuming the leadership of the Holy Spirit, this is a good time to give it a "shot" and present the gospel.[2]

Drawing the Net through Evangelistic Events/Presentations

Evangelistic events are easily one of the best approaches to gathering people and allowing for both personal and mass appeals to the gospel. The problem is that they are usually more geared to the "come and hear" model rather than "go and tell." This can be altered by having some of the events off site at a local park, etc. There is also the issue of follow-up and discipleship.

Nevertheless, evangelistic events do provide opportunities for widespread church participation. There is also the "fish in a barrel" syndrome, where sharing one's faith becomes easier in a controlled setting. Some of these events are:

Evangelistic Block Parties

Evangelistic block parties are some of the easiest and most effective outreach events. They generally consist of a registration table (everyone gets registered or they do not receive tickets for lunch or the opportunity to win door prizes), popcorn machine, snow cone machine, cotton candy machine, helium tanks for lots of balloons, plus plenty of tables, chairs, and pop-up tents in case of bad weather. You can also use a grill for the hotdogs, hamburgers, BBQ chicken, etc., or you can prepare nachos, chili, you name it.

There are typically seven to ten simple games, moonwalks, face painting, etc. It can be done on the church campus or even at a local park. Church members usually blitz the community several times in the weeks leading up to the party, and always on the morning of the event. As people arrive they are greeted by smiling Christians of all ages who assist in directing the families to different events.

In many cases, these simple encounters lead to divine opportunities to share a brief testimony and in some cases, to make a gospel presentation. This is why it is imperative to train all the workers ahead of time. It is also important to plan the follow-up immediately (within the first three to five days) with every registered nonchurch member.

For more information pertaining to Evangelistic Block Parties, go to www.namb.net and do a search for Block Parties. For a free copy of the *Block Party Manual,* go to www.innovatechurch.us under "outreach."

Sports Evangelism

One of the most effective approaches in evangelism is the process that missiologist's call contextualization. By nature, contextualization is the adapting of evangelistic methodologies into culture without compromising the essential truths of the gospel. It is simply learning to clothe the message so that it can best be understood by the recipients in that culture. This usually includes things such as language and dress, but in contemporary culture it should also include the avenue of sports.

For instance, consider for a moment the power and influence of sports in American society. In many ways, it is the language of contemporary culture. Almost everyone can recognize the distinctive theme tones of ESPN's "Sports Center," or at least they are aware of the Super Bowl, World Series, Olympics, or the World Cup. Though it can easily be a distraction away from spiritual matters, sports have also become a cultural language that demands "contextual" attention.

Instead of criticizing families for over involvement, maybe it is time to start commissioning. Think about it: what if your church teamed up with young parents who are already involved in local soccer, baseball, softball, or football leagues? Rather than instilling guilty feelings about missing Wednesday or Sunday evening services, how about commissioning these parents as missionaries to the local athletic fields?

The approach could include an actual time of church-based praying for the families before sending them out. The church can then keep the parents accountable through weekly contacts and encourage them to make a prayer list of all the team players and their families. These lists could then be sent back to the church's prayer room or dispersed among small groups for further attention.

Congregations could also give the parents a small sum of money ($150 to $200) so they can stock up on after-game snacks for the entire team. That will easily make them the most popular parents among the players. Then instruct the parents to tell the coaches that they are welcome to utilize the church's facilities for their end of the season banquet. The church may also choose to provide the meal as well as volunteers to serve the parents and the players. In the end, it will be a great opportunity to demonstrate Christ's love by reaching out to young families, many of which know very little about spiritual matters.

In addition, you might also consider forsaking local "church leagues" in basketball, softball, etc. This was the case one summer while serving as senior pastor of a congregation in Texas. The church invaded the local "city" league and as a result, they eventually picked up several new families as well as numerous new believers. You can even provide free sodas for the other teams after the games.

Sports are a great tool for effective evangelism. From church sponsored three-on-three basketball tournaments and soccer clinics, to working with FCA chapters through local schools, a wise church will utilize sports as a "contextual" tool to impact the community for Christ.

For additional information relating to local church sports ministries, go to www.upward.com. For a comprehensive "free" downloadable manual on sports ministries, go to www.victorlee.org/sportsmanual. For golf, go to www.inhisgripgolf.com. A general sports Web site is www.sport.org.

Seasonal and Gender Related Events

Another effective approach to harvesting is through seasonal events such as Christmas and Easter programs. This can also be done through July 4 celebrations or fall festivals. These activities are yearly events at Thomas Road Baptist Church in Lynchburg, Virginia. They draw large audiences and are very intentional in their evangelistic approach.

In addition, as far as gender-related events, Mother's Day celebrations and Mother-Daughter Banquets are always effective. For the men, wild game suppers (or "beast feasts"), motorcycle rallies and car shows will always draw a crowd and provide plenty of evangelistic opportunities, especially when combined with block-party type activities. "Back to School" events and "fall festivals" (Halloween) are also great opportunities to impact the community for Christ. Each of these approaches provides easy ways for the congregation to invite people for the purpose of evangelism.

For more helpful information relating to the Easter, Christmas, and July 4th activities, go to www.trbc.org; or go to www.inno vatechurch.us under "outreach" for more creative ideas and "free" downloadable event manuals relating to Halloween, Thanksgiving, Christmas, and Valentine's Day. For information relating to the wild game feasts and sportsman type outreaches, go to www.chris tiansportsman.com or www.legacyoutdoorministry.com.

Good Approaches to Sharing One's Faith

Along with the evangelistic events, there are several very good informational approaches to sharing one's faith. Some of these are:

- *Share Jesus Without Fear*—A simple approach that uses a series of probing questions combined with the Bible that takes the fear out of sharing (www. sharejesuswithoutfear.com),
- *FAITH*—An easy approach that utilizes the acrostic FAITH to remember the gospel presentation. It seeks to tie everything back through the Sunday school (www. lifeway.com).
- *Got Life*—An easy outline that utilizes the acrostic LIFE. It has a strong apologetics application within the overall presentation (www.gotlife.org).

- *The Way of the Master*—Utilizes the "Ten Commandments" and a series of probing questions as a basis to establish "lostness" and present Christ (www. thewayofthemaster.com).
- *Evangecube*—Great visual approach to sharing one's faith. Utilizes a small cube that is rotated to reveal a picture of the gospel (www.simplysharejesus.com).
- *God's Special Plan*—A simple yet well prepared presentation of the gospel for children (www.kidzplace.org).

Staying on Track Strategically

Each of the approaches mentioned in this chapter will be effective, to varying degrees, in any church situation. However, there must always be a dependence on the Holy Spirit and a foundation of fervent prayer. Without a collective passion for Christ and a willingness to surrender one's desires to that of the Father through prayer, we will be playing musical chairs through our evangelistic programs.

God's desire is to create a multiplication movement that magnifies Christ through His disciples living as His Church. This should result in natural conversion growth of His body. To accomplish this, the church leader must not minimize the need to strategically apply the principles of the harvest. It is never enough to adopt a program or event as a stand-alone outreach if it is not strategically linked to a larger vision that mobilizes the church to multiply through both new believers and new congregations.

Notes

1. Alvin L. Reid and David A. Wheeler, *Servanthood Evangelism Manual* (North American Mission Board, 1999), 7.
2. Jack Smith, *Friends Forever* (Home Mission Board, 1994).

CHURCH
PLANTING

CHAPTER 10

The Why of Church Planting

by Dave Earley

As a pastor the one constant that kept me going was the never disappointing honor of working with God to help people come to Christ, and the always fresh privilege of birthing a new church. This chapter is written with one purpose: to convince you and your church to get into God's nursery. I want to help motivate, stimulate, and educate you to play a much greater role in cooperating with God in His big plan to reach this world for Jesus Christ through the experience of church starting.

I am going to assume that you have already had your heart broken by the billions of unreached people on our planet, both inside and outside our borders. I want to rekindle your passion for reaching your city and region with the gospel and touching this nation with the message of Jesus Christ. I want to spur you to consider leading your church to become what I call "a multiplication center," by starting churches that will subsequently plant other churches in North America. Our continent is, in fact, starving for the hope of the gospel of Christ.

Let's examine eleven critical points regarding our call to reach out with the gospel to our nation through church-planting efforts.

North America desperately needs more churches.

The questions are common: "Why plant churches in North America when so many churches are dead or dying? Shouldn't the focus be on returning struggling churches to health?" "Why plant churches in North America when so many churches have so many empty seats?" "Shouldn't churches work to fill all those seats before we start other churches?" "Is it worth the time, money, and effort to train church planters?" "Are new churches really needed?"

The answer to the last two questions is a resounding, "Yes!" Let's examine some data that shows just how much America needs new churches. As unbelievable is it may seem, recent research indicates that there are now more than two-hundred million nonchurched people in America, making our nation one of the largest "unchurched" countries in the world. Author Justice Anderson has stated, "The American church is in the midst of one of the largest mission fields in the world today. Only three other nations—China, India and Indonesia—have more lost people."[1]

Did you know that in 1987 the number of evangelicals in Asia surpassed the number of evangelicals in North America? And did you know that in 1991 the number of evangelicals in Asia surpassed the number of evangelicals *in the entire Western World*?[2]

In spite of the rise of American megachurches, no county in our nation has a greater churched population than it did ten years ago.[3] During the last ten years, combined communicant membership of all Protestant denominations declined by 9.5 percent (4,498,242), while the national population increased by 11.4 percent (24,153,000).[4]

In 1990 20.4 percent of Americans attended church on any given Sunday. By the year 2000 only 18.7 percent attended church. This percentage is still in decline and if this trend is not turned around, it will not be long before only 6 percent of Americans attend church each week. According to Dave Olson's research, the recent increase in the number of churches is only about one-eighth of what is needed to keep up with population growth.[5]

As a result, even though America has more people, it has fewer churches per person than at any time in her history. And while the number of churches in America has increased by 50 percent in the last century, the population has increased a staggering 300 percent.[6] There are now nearly 60 percent fewer churches per 10,000 Americans than there were in 1920!

Table 1: Number of Churches per Americans[7]

1920   27 churches existed for every 10,000 Americans.
1950   17 churches existed for every 10,000 Americans.
1996   11 churches existed for every 10,000 Americans.

North America is rapidly becoming a post-Christian nation.

A couple of years ago, my youngest son came home from his first day of high school in a suburb of Columbus, Ohio. I asked him who was at his lunch table. "It was interesting, Dad," he said. "There was a Muslim, a Buddhist, a Mormon, a Catholic, a Jew, a Christian friend, and some kids that don't consider themselves anything." Thirty years ago he might have answered, "A Methodist, a Presbyterian, a Catholic, a Baptist, and a kid whose dad works on Sundays." Times have certainly changed, even in the Midwest. For Americans my age and even somewhat younger, the America we grew up in is not the America in which we now live.

Any student of the American culture knows that in spite of the vast amounts of time, energy, and money spent to influence the political process, Christian values are quickly disappearing from our culture. Honesty, morality, and integrity are concepts that have been either redefined or completely discounted. As our culture has become increasingly less welcoming to the Judeo-Christian principles that are the bedrock of our nation, many in our nation have simultaneously become more hostile to evangelical Christianity. One of the key reasons for this is that we have proportionately less evangelical Christians in our culture.

Dr. Aubrey Malphurs, professor of pastoral ministries at Dallas Theological Seminary and head of the Malphurs Group, has made a wise observation on this culture shift. "Essentially," he says, "what was a churched, supposedly Christian culture has become an un-churched, post-Christian culture. People in our culture are not antichurch; they simply view the church as irrelevant to their lives."[8] It is evident that we must plant churches so that Americans will once again see the church as relevant to their lives and families.

As America increasingly moves from a Christian to a post-Christian, postmodern culture, it will become increasingly important to plant new churches to present the timeless truths of the gospel in a new and timely manner. We must put new wine in new wineskins. A new army of well-trained, effectively taught church planters is essential to win back the North American continent for Christ in the twenty-first century.

Longtime church growth expert Lyle Schaller observes, "There is not a congregation that possesses the ability and the financial resources to attract, reach, and respond to the needs of all the residents of the community."[9] What many evangelicals fail to realize is that there exists a flawed understanding that the United States and Canada are already evangelized. While there is abundant access to Christian information, many unchurched persons in North America are amazingly untouched by the evangelical culture (or maybe subculture) because the Christian community is too often incapable of providing a culturally relevant gospel witness.[10]

"The single most effective evangelistic methodology under heaven is planting new churches."

The above statement was made several decades ago by Peter Wagner, president of the Global Harvest Ministries. I believe the statement is as true today as it has ever been. For example, one American denomination recently found that 80 percent of its converts came to Christ in churches less than two years old.[11] Further, baptism rates for new churches are three- to ten-times higher than existing churches.

New churches reach lost people more effectively than existing churches. Churches that are more than fifteen years of age win an average of only three people to Christ per year for every one hundred church members. Churches between three and fifteen years old conversely win an average of five people to Christ per year for every one hundred church members. But churches less than three years of age win an average of ten people to Christ per year for every one hundred church members.[12] Truly, when the church exhales churches, it inhales converts.

New churches reach new people; existing churches reach existing people. This is true because most new churches are focused as "missional" entities, meaning they typically concentrate on reaching the lost and fulfilling the Great Commission. But too many existing churches have turned inward and have forgotten why they exist. New Christians reach lost people; established Christians fellowship with Christian friends. After a person gets saved, they generally have a network of unchurched friends they want to evangelize. But after they have been saved a few years, they have either reached their lost friends or they no longer spend much time with them. Their ability to reach people through friendships drastically declines.

America needs new churches if the Great Commission is to be fulfilled, because new churches are noticeably more effective at reaching lost people than existing churches. Church growth expert Win Arn states, "Today, of the approximately 350,000 churches in America, four out of five are either plateaued or declining . . . Many churches begin a plateau or slow decline about their fifteenth to eighteenth year. Eighty to 85 percent of the churches in America are on the downside of this cycle. Of the 15 percent that are growing, 14 percent are growing from transfer, rather than conversion growth."[13] This means that only 1 percent of the churches in our nation are making a significant impact regarding our responsibility to reach lost people for Jesus Christ. It is painfully clear that we need more new churches.

"It is easier to give birth than to raise the dead."

This statement was a trumpet call of the great church-planting efforts of the Baptist Bible Fellowship of the 1950s. This great theme prompted a young graduate of Baptist Bible College named Jerry Falwell to start Thomas Road Baptist Church in his hometown in 1956, along with a handful of believers. It was also the theme that motivated me to launch New Life Church in Gahanna/ Columbus, Ohio, when I was just twenty-six years old and a recent graduate of Liberty University and Liberty Baptist Theological Seminary. I understood that I did not have the experience, wisdom, wiring, or patience to lead an existing church in its retooling efforts to reach the lost members of my generation. So I started a new church that was better designed to speak the language of the unchurched. While we started out being smaller than most of the existing churches in our suburb, we quickly outgrew and reached more lost people than all of them. I say this not to brag, but to show how new churches can uniquely impact a community. At this new church, we had no traditional barriers to hurdle, no mind-set strongholds to tear down, no committees to please, and no inward focus to circumvent. We could simply focus on the task at hand: winning the lost at any cost.

Maybe your calling is to be what I call a "transitioner" at an existing church. In this, I mean you are attempting to shift old assumptions regarding evangelism so that you can reach out to your community in new ways. If that is the case, may God bless you! I hope you are able to lead your church in becoming a true multiplication center that is also dedicated to launching new churches all over the world. However, it is important to note that incredible amounts of time, energy, and effort can be expended trying to transition existing churches, and some have done so with great success. While it can sometimes be done, we need to accept the fact that it is indeed easier to give birth than to raise the dead.

"The Great Commission is church planting."

You cannot call your church a "Great Commission church" until you are heavily involved in starting new churches. Any Great Commission initiative that does not result in the forming of new churches misses the mark. Let me explain. After Jesus rose from the dead, He laid out for His followers the desires He most deeply longed for them to fulfill. Repeatedly Jesus gave a command that has become known as the Great Commission. The writers of the Gospels record Jesus giving His Great Commission five times. The fullest statement is found in Matthew 28: "Then Jesus came near and said to them, 'All authority has been given to Me in heaven and on earth. Go, therefore, and make disciples of all nations, baptizing them in the name of the Father and of the Son and of the Holy Spirit, teaching them to observe everything I have commanded you. And remember, I am with you always, to the end of the age'" (Matt. 28:18–20; see also Mark 16:15–16; Luke 24:46–48; John 20:21; Acts 1:8).

After examining the Great Commission, the question that begs to be answered is: How does God expect His followers to implement it? The obvious answer is: by planting churches.

Church planting involves all the elements of fulfilling the Great Commission. New churches are the result of Christians invading a culture, preaching the gospel, baptizing believers, and training disciples.

After the disciples heard the five offerings of the Great Commission, what did they do to obey it? The book of Acts reveals that they started new churches.

Ed Stetzer of Global Church Advancement has planted churches in New York, Pennsylvania, and Georgia and transitioned declining churches in Indiana and Georgia. He writes, "New Testament Christians acted out these commands as any spiritually healthy, obedient believers would; they planted more New Testament churches."[14] He concludes, "The Great Commission *is* church planting."[15]

The way the first followers of Jesus carried out the Great Commission directly resulted in the planting of churches. Peter (and others) preached the gospel (see Acts 2:14–36), the people were baptized (see Acts 2:37–41), and the baptized believers were immediately incorporated into the life of obeying what Jesus had taught (see Acts 2:42–47). The ultimate fulfillment of the Great Commission was, is, and will always be church planting. This is how I can say that your church is not fulfilling the Great Commission until it is actively involved in starting new churches.

Church planting expands the kingdom of God.

Jesus told us that the top priority on our lives was to be God's kingdom (see Matt. 6:33). He taught us to pray for the coming of God's kingdom (see Matt. 6:9–10). He said that unless someone is born again, they cannot even see the kingdom of God (see John 3:3–7). God's passion is that His kingdom spread to all peoples. His plan is that His kingdom increases through church planting.

Fred Herron makes this case following a careful study of the Word of God: "God's heart for the expansion of his kingdom is revealed throughout the Old and New Testament. God intends the church to proclaim and demonstrate the kingdom so that his kingdom will spread to every people group on the earth. The passion in God's heart for the expansion of his kingdom is a desire for all nations to glorify God the eternal King. He has given the church a kingly commission to go into the entire world and make disciples who are loyal worshippers of the King. The heart of God for kingdom expansion is the foundation for planting new churches."[16]

Authors David W. Shrenk and Ervin R. Stutzman also see the kingdom link with church planting. They have written, "Church planting is thus the most urgent business of humankind. It is through the creation (or planting) of churches that God's kingdom is extended into communities which have not been touched by the precious surprise of the presence of the kingdom of God in their midst."[17]

Every time we start a new church in a new community, we are being a part of the answer to that prayer. Every time a new church reaches a person for Christ, a new citizen has been added to the kingdom of heaven. I fear that there are too many pastors in our nation that have allowed a passion for church growth to supersede a passion for the kingdom of God. It is refreshing to know, however, that there are many pastors and church leaders that are more excited about building God's kingdom than building their own kingdoms.

Church planting is being on a mission with God.

Missio Dei is a Latin phrase that has been helpful in reminding the church that its mission is not the invention, responsibility, or program of human origin, but flows from the character and purposes of God.[18] Historically the term *mission* was used to describe the acts of God, rather than the activities of churches. Mission is not something the church does for God; it is rather the church getting in sync with the heart of God and cooperating with the activity of God.

According to noted church planting coach and professor Tom Jones, "God's nature is at the root of mission. The living God portrayed in the Bible is a sending God. He sends because of His love for the world (see John 3:16). He sent Abraham from his home into the unknown, promising to bless the world through him if he obeyed (see Gen. 12:1–3). God sent Joseph into Egypt to help preserve God's people during a time of famine (see Gen. 45:4–8). When the time had fully come, God sent His Son. Later, the Father and the Son sent the Spirit on Pentecost (see Gal. 4:4–6; John 14:26; 15:26; 16:7; Acts 2:33). Finally Christ sends His church (see Matt. 28:19–20)."[19]

Jones adds, "The most efficient way to fulfill the total mission of a sent church is the multiplication of local churches. . . . Every local church should consider itself a center for world mission."[20]

The late Swiss theologian Emil Brunner has memorably stated, "The Church exists by mission, just as fire exists by burning."[21] The church of God is to be on mission with God. When a church ceases to be on this mission, in a real sense, it ceases. David Bosch concurs, stating, "It is impossible to talk about church without at the same time talking about mission. Because God is a missionary God, God's people are missionary people. The church's mission is not secondary to its being: the church exists in being sent and building up itself for its mission."[22]

Our God is the Missionary who sent His Word, His Son, and His Spirit into the world. God is the One who defines, directs, energizes, and accomplishes mission here in our midst. Therefore, God is the Originator, Catalyst, Architect, and Engineer of church planting. Church planting is merely cooperating with Him in fulfilling His global mission initiative.

Church planting brings the hands and heart of Jesus into the lives of needy people.

Two thousand years ago the miraculous act of God's incarnation (taking human flesh) did not merely reveal Him as a man; it also served to model evangelism to mankind. When the Word became flesh, believers learned the importance of enfolding proclamation into incarnation. It is not enough to merely tell the gospel; it must be lived out with and before people in Christian communities.

The New Testament way of "living Jesus" with, and before, hurting people was and still is through His body, the church. A healthy church is the body of Christ on earth. Establishing a new church brings the hands and heart of Jesus into the lives of needy people.

In 2003 Roscoe and Maryanna Lilly moved to Clifton Park, New York, and began serving the community by washing car windows in the mall parking lot and cleaning public restrooms without charge. As a result, the Northstar Church was born with a handful of people. They are passionate about being the hands and feet of Jesus, making Him relevant to their community. They exist to show God's love in such a way that people will exchange ordinary living for an extraordinary life through the power of Jesus Christ. Last year, the young and growing congregation clocked more than sixteen hundred community service hours. They say their ministry embodies a formula they call S.A.L.T., which is:

Seeing people the way Jesus saw them;

Accepting people the way Jesus accepted them;

Loving people the way Jesus loved them;

Touching people the way Jesus touched them.

"Be fruitful and multiply!"

The very first command in the Bible is "be fruitful and multiply" (Gen. 1:22 NASB). For plants, this commandment meant they must reproduce plants. For Adam and Eve, it meant they should bear children. And for churches, this command means to plant new churches.

Dr. Elmer Towns, who is involved in this InnovateChurch project, and Douglas Porter write, "The Church is a living body. Just as everything that's alive will grow and reproduce, so your church should be growing and reproducing itself by starting another new church. Just as God originally created all living things to reproduce, that is, 'according to its kind' (Gen. 1:11–12, 21), so your church can double its ministry by planting another church."[23]

Some time ago there was a display at the Museum of Science and Industry in Chicago. It featured a checkerboard with one grain of wheat on the first square, two grains on the second square, four on the third, then eight, sixteen, thirty-two, sixty-four, and so on. At the end of the board there were so many grains of wheat on one square they were spilling over into neighboring squares. And here the demonstration stopped. Above the checkerboard display was a question: "At this rate of doubling every square, how much grain would be on the checkerboards by the sixty-fourth square?" To find the answer to this riddle, you punched a button on the console in front of you, and the answer flashed on a little screen above the board: "Enough to cover the entire subcontinent of India 50 feet deep."[24]

The problem in North America is that we have been working hard to add converts when we should have been investing our energy and effort into multiplying churches. The population grows through multiplication, but we have focused on addition. If we have any hope of turning the tide, we must invest our lives in multiplying churches. The *slow* process of multiplying churches is the *fastest* way to fulfill the Great Commission.

Multiplication may be costly, and in the initial stages much slower than addition, but in the long run it is the most effective way of accomplishing Christ's Great Commission. In fact, it is the *only* way. Your church cannot call itself a Great Commission church until it becomes a church multiplication center.

Storm the gates!

Too many Christians and churches have gone into hiding. We have retreated to our Christian ghettoes, going to our Christian schools, listening to our Christian radio stations, and hanging out with only our Christian friends. As the culture moves further from biblical values, we retreat further from the culture. And it breaks the heart of Jesus.

In Matthew 16, Jesus was giving His disciples an opportunity to grasp a deep understanding of His identity and, thereby, a clearer comprehension of their destiny. In verse 18, He gives a statement which has become known as the Great Promise: "I tell you that you are Peter, and on this rock I will build my church, and the gates of Hades will not overcome it" (NIV).

This promise clearly states that, because Jesus is the church builder, the church is an unstoppable force that must storm the gates of hell! We are not to be passive cowards who are hunkered down in fear of the world around us. We are to be a militant, aggressive army on the offensive for God, working to rescue captives from hell.

Nothing causes the enemy to sit up and take notice as much as the start of a new church that is willing to penetrate the culture, identify with the captives and kick down the very gates of hell, if that is what it takes. Every church planter I know has come face to face with severe spiritual warfare. But they also tell me that the trials they have faced have been small prices to pay in exchange for the great joy of seeing souls set free.

"Give and it shall be given unto you."

As church leaders, we are quick to point out to our people the principle that "you cannot outgive God." We tell them that, if they will give God one-tenth of their income, God will stretch the remaining 90 percent. We encourage them to give God their first-fruits because He will bless them for it (see Prov. 3:9–10). We also quote to them Luke 6:38: "Give and it will be given to you; a good measure—pressed down, shaken together, and running over—will be poured into your lap. For with the measure you use, it will be measured back to you."

Yet, ask the same church leaders to send out a team of their best members to start a new church and they will cough uncomfortably and try to change the subject. They will say that their church is not yet big enough to plant a daughter church. They will balk at the thought of "giving away people." They would never consider giving up one-tenth of their members to plant a new church.

That attitude seems inconsistent with God's promise to reward our faithfulness to Him, doesn't it? The goal should be to build God's kingdom, not one's own kingdom. Besides, God blesses generosity in all phases of the Christian life—not just in financial giving. For example, Leith Anderson, senior pastor of Wooddale Church in Eden Prairie, Minnesota, has led his church to plant several new churches in the last decade. He says that every time his church has sent out people to start a new church, God has consequently sent that number, plus more, to replace those who set out from the mother church.[25]

In my role as a senior pastor, I was initially hesitant to get involved in church planting. But God allowed me to eventually see that all my reasons for my wavering were only excuses. I then began to more intentionally send out members who started daughter churches. When we sent out the first group of families, it hurt to see them go. They were leaders, tithers, and friends. I had no idea then what God had in store for our church because we willingly sent out these members. That year, our church attendance and giving grew at a rate that more than replaced the numbers we had sent out. Again and again, God gave back to us when we gave to build His kingdom. We would take in more families, baptize more people, and sense the pleasure of God.

Most pastors want their church members to tithe one-tenth, or more, of their income. What a difference it would make if every church in America sent out a tithe of their people every few years to plant new churches, as well.

Two Questions

If you can read half of these eleven reasons without being deeply stirred about getting more involved in church planting, you may be spiritually asleep, or even dead. I want to conclude this chapter by asking you two important questions about starting new churches:

1. If not you, who?
2. If not now, when?

Notes:

1. Justice Anderson, in *Missiology: An Introduction to the Foundations, History, and Strategies of Word Missions,* ed. John Mark Terry, Ebbie Smith, Justice Anderson (Nashville: Broadman & Holman, 1998), 243.

2. William Craig, Reasonable Faith, "Subject: Molinism, the Unevangelized, and Cultural Chauvinism" http://www.reasonablefaith.org/site/News2?page=NewsArticle&id=5681; (accessed January 21, 2008).

3. Ron Sylvia, *Starting High Definition Churches* (Ocala, FL: High Definition Resources, 2004), 26.

4. Tom Clegg, "How to Plant a Church for the 21st Century," seminar materials, 1997, author's collection, Gahanna, Ohio.

5. Dave Olsen, http://www.theamericanchurch.org.

6. Bill Easum, "The Easum Report," March 2003; available from http://www.easum.com/church.htm; Internet.

7. Tom Clegg and Warren Bird, *Lost in America: How You and Your Church Can Impact the World Next Door* (Loveland, CA: Group Publishing, 2001), 30.

8. Aubrey Malphurs, *Planting Growing Churches for the Twenty-First Century* (Grand Rapids: Baker, 1992), 27.

9. Lyle Schaller, *44 Questions for Church Planters* (Nashville, TN: Abingdon Press, 1991), 43.

10. Ed Stetzer, *Planting New Churches in a Postmodern Age* (Nashville, TN: Broadman & Holman, 2003), 9.

11. Ralph Moore, *Starting a New Church* (Ventura, CA: Regal Book, 2002), 3.

12. Brian McNichol, quoted in "Churches Die With Dignity," *Christianity Today,* 14 January 1991, 69.

13. Win Arn, *The Pastor's Manual for Effective Ministry* (Monrovia, CA: 1988), 41.

14. Stetzer, *Planting New Churches,* 37.

15. Ibid., 35.

16. Fred Herron, *Expanding God's Kingdom Through Church Planting* (Lincoln, NE: iUniverse, 2003), 19.

17. David W. Shrenk and Ervin R. Stutzman, *Creating Communities of the Kingdom* (Scottsdale, PA: Herald Press, 1988), 23.

18. Stuart Murray, *Church Planting: Laying Foundations* (Scottsdale, PA: Herald Press, 2001), 39.

19. Tom Jones, *Church Planting from the Ground Up* (Joplin, MO: College Press, 2004), 10.

20. Ibid., 16.

21. Wilbert R. Shenk, *Write the Vision* (Harrisburg, PA: Trinity Press, 1995), 87.

22. David J. Bosch, *Believing in the Future* (Harrisburg, PA: Trinity Press, 1995), 32.

23. Elmer L. Towns and Douglas Porter, *Churches That Multiply* (Kansas City, MO: Beacon Hill Press, 2003), 7.

24. Walter Henrichsen, *Disciples Are Made, Not Born* (Wheaton, IL: Victor Books, 1974), 143.

25. Leith Anderson, Senior Pastor of Wooddale Church, Eden Prairie, MN, informal interview by author, June 2002, author's notes, Gahanna, Ohio.

CHAPTER 11

The How of Church Parenting

by Dave Earley

Five years ago I met a man from Nigeria named Sam. As we talked during our initial conversation, I asked Sam why he had come to America. I was shocked by his answer. He said, "I am a missionary to America." He went on to tell me, "God has sent me here to bring the gospel and start churches."

Let me assure you that Pastor Sam is not the only missionary to America. For more than two hundred years, Western nations sent missionaries to Africa, South America, and Asia. Today, in a remarkable and astonishing turn of events, the world has begun sending missionaries here to preach the gospel, make disciples, and plant churches. This news should send a collective shiver down the spine of every Christian in this nation!

After meeting Pastor Sam, I left with a greater resolution to participate more fully in the job of sending out missionaries within our own nation. I determined that if I did nothing else the rest of my life, I would get involved in planting churches in North America. This has become my heart's great desire, and I want to encourage more pastors and more churches to get involved in this critical effort as well.

The most effective method of evangelism is church planting.

The most effective method of church planting is church *parenting*.[1]

I was recently speaking with a pastor who leads a healthy, growing church. He said, "OK, I am convinced that God wants our church to be involved in planting churches. Now what? Tell me how to do it."

"I am glad you asked," I said with a grin. "Let me tell you several practical steps you can take to get involved in church parenting." And in this chapter I would like to share with pastors and church leaders the same practical steps I outlined to my pastor friend that day. I pray that these steps will invigorate your soul and your ministry. I further pray that you will catch the vision of church planting and see the urgent need for this effort in our nation.

STEP 1: Cast the vision of multiplication to your leaders.

Effective ministry rises and falls on leadership; effective leadership is born out of vision. Successful leaders are not only able to *see* the vision, they are able to *share* that vision. No church leader has ever led their church to plant churches without first casting the vision to do so.

Here are some key ways in which pastors and church leaders can cast the vision for planting churches in our nation.

Start by Painting the Big Picture

People are largely unaware of the need to plant more churches in America. Christians in our nation need to know that America is actually the third-largest mission field on the planet. They further need to understand that North America is rapidly becoming as post-Christian as Western Europe.

When casting the vision for church planting, use the statistics, quotes, and principles offered in the previous chapter in your teachings. I have never shared that information with serious Christians who did not walk away understanding that we do need to plant many more effective churches in North America.

Show the Need in Your Area

Nothing is dynamic until it becomes specific. You need to help your church leaders begin to understand the specific need for more churches in your own community. Let me suggest two simple exercises you can use to help your staff and leaders begin to see the need.

People with No Seat This Sunday

A. Record the population in your area: _____

B. List the churches in the area, the number of people they can seat in their worship facilities, and how many Sunday services they hold each week.

Church	Number of Seats	Weekend Services	Total seats available for worship each weekend

Total: _____

C. If every person in your area decided to go to church this Sunday, how many people would not have a seat? Subtract B (the total number of available seats for churchgoers in your city) from A (the number of people in your city) in order to determine the answer to this question.

Our church (New Life Church Gahanna Ohio) was in a town of 30,000 people. There were 20 churches in our town with a combined seating capacity of 9,700 people. That meant that if everyone in our town decided to go to church on any given Sunday, 20,300 people would not have had a seat.

The Western world is the only major segment of the planet in which Christianity is not growing.[2] In fact, church attendance in North America continues to plummet, dropping from 60 percent attendance after WWII, to 49 percent in 1991, to the current 18 percent.[3]

Another exercise you can use to help your staff and members catch the vision of church planting is to figure out how many people in your community are not involved in church on any given Sunday.

We found that even on Easter Sunday, two-thirds of the people in our town did not attend church. On any given Sunday, the weekly worship attendance was about 20 percent of our town's population. That means that with a population of 30,000, the attendance on any given Sunday was about 6,000 people, meaning 24,000 did not attend church. Further, 1.3 million people lived in our metropolitan area. If 20 percent attended church on any given Sunday, that means that more than a million people did not.

On Any Given Sunday

A. Record the population in your area: _____

B. List the churches in the area and the number of people they had attend church on average per week last month.

Church	Number of people attending church per week

Total: _____

C. How many people attended church per week? How many did not attend? Subtract B (the number of people attending church per week), from A (the number of people in your area) in order to determine the answer to this question.

$$A - B = C$$

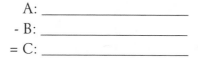

A: _____
- B: _____
= C: _____

Pray!

Thomas Road Baptist Church founder Jerry Falwell used to say, "Nothing of eternal significance ever happens apart from prayer."[4] Prayer uniquely links our hearts with God's hearts. Take every opportunity you can to pray about the need to plant churches. When you pray publicly during your weekend worship services or during deacons meetings, begin to mention the need for more churches.

Specifically you can lead your church to pray for eyes to see the harvest. Also, pray for the future soil to be cultivated and for the workers to be raised up. Finally, ask Jesus to give you His vision, direction, timing, and blessing for church planting.

STEP 2: Challenge the culture of your church.

The task of an effective leader is to closely monitor the culture of their church. Whenever it strays from the scriptural ideal of being a healthy, growing, multiplying army for God, we need to challenge the culture that permitted the demise in the first place.

Refuse to Give in to Excuses

Often when pastors begin to probe their church with the concept of becoming more involved in church planting, they encounter reasons why it would be easier to not be involved. Are any of these excuses holding your church back?

Four Common Reasons (Excuses) for Not Being Involved in Church Planting

1. "We aren't big enough yet."

I find that many pastors have some ideal size their church needs to get to *before* they will even think about planting churches. This apparent magic number is usually (and conveniently) about twice their current size. If their attendance is 100, they think they need to wait until their attendance reaches 200. But this type of thinking is about as reasonable as when people say they will begin to tithe when they begin to make more money. It just doesn't work that way.

The reality is that a church of any size can be involved in helping to plant new churches. Churches merely need to be willing to get involved. Many new churches are, from their very beginning, placing multiplication into their collective DNA, and they are successfully starting daughter churches within three years of their own launch.

Even small, brand new churches can pray. They can send teams of people to pass out literature or send a crew to watch the nursery when the embryonic church has a planning meeting. They can take up a special offering and partner in any number of ways with other congregations to help launch the new church.

2. "We aren't healthy enough to start new churches."

While this may sound logical at first, we need to realize that helping to start new churches is something God wants to use to help your church *become* healthy. Nothing is as beneficial for a struggling church as getting the congregation's eyes off themselves and onto helping others. Nothing helps a church get healthy like getting involved on the front lines of fulfilling the Great Commission.

3. "We might fail."

This excuse flows out of a failure to comprehend Matthew 16:18, a pivotal verse wherein we see Jesus make an authoritative and powerful promise: "I will build My church, and the forces of Hades will not overpower it." Jesus is the church builder; not us. If we try to do it all in our strength, we will certainly fail. However, if we are cooperating with Him in His work, we cannot fail. Instead of letting a fear of failure cause us to be passive and unreceptive to the need of church planting, we must allow the apparent need to drive us to pray as hard as we can, learn as fast as we can and work as hard as we can to bring about needed change.

4. "We cannot afford it."

I would be amiss if I led you to believe that starting new churches won't cost you anything. Let me state it very simply: Successfully starting new churches will cost you time, money, manpower, attention, energy, and prayers. It will put your church on the enemy's radar screen and make you the target for genuine spiritual warfare.

Yes, church parenting is costly. Yet God promises to bless those who give: "Give, and it will be given to you; a good measure, pressed down, shaken together, and running over—will be poured into your lap. For with the measure you use, it will be measured back to you" (Luke 6:38).

We like to use this promise to generally encourage our people to be generous with their resources. As I noted in the previous chapter, we frequently tell them, "You cannot outgive God." Yet, we are often simultaneously stingy when it comes to leading our churches to give away manpower and money to plant daughter churches. God promises to bless those who give. And there is no limit to how much He can give back to churches that follow His call.

Four times in six years our church planted a daughter church. During the four years we gave away money and teams of people to launch a new church, our baptism rates increased, our giving rates increased and our attendance increased. We discovered that you cannot outgive God. It was a true lesson in miraculous living.

Churches that plant other churches have a renewed zeal for evangelism and have a deepened passion for the Great Commission. They learn new strategies of effective evangelism from planting daughter churches.

The human body is remarkably designed. When you give blood, your body will quickly replace all of it. The church is the body of Christ. Similarly, when we give away leaders, members, and money to plant a daughter church, God quickly replaces those leaders, members, and finances with new ones. You can't outgive God.

On paper, planting a new church may seem like a steep endeavor. But when you consider the fact that people are going to hell because they are not hearing the gospel, you cannot afford *not* to plant churches. When you consider the need to keep your church outwardly focused, you cannot refuse to get involved.

And when you consider the fact that you can literally never outgive God, you cannot afford not to help start new churches.

Build Multiplication Values into Your Church Culture

Before a church can effectively "mother" a daughter church, there often needs to be a shift to multiplication values. The left side of the following chart shows several common church values. The right side reveals biblical values that are needed for multiplication. As you examine the chart, note the values in which your church needs to grow so that it becomes a church-planting multiplication center.

Necessary Multiplication Value Shifts

Fear	to	Faith
Territorial	to	Kingdom mind-set
Safety and Selfishness	to	Sacrificial Generosity
Isolation	to	Involvement and Partnership
Complacency	to	Commitment
Laziness	to	Learning and Leadership

How to Build Multiplication Values into Your Church

1. Model Multiplication Values

Before a church will ever adopt multiplication values, the leaders need to model those values. Our congregations are more likely to do what they see before they will do what they hear. Let me ask you:

- Are you a person of active, growing faith?
- Are you more interested in building God's kingdom, or your own?
- Do you practice sacrificial generosity?

- Do you partner with others to accomplish God-sized goals?
- Are you a person of deep personal commitment?
- Are you always learning and improving as a leader?
- Of the essential multiplication values (faith, kingdom mind-set, sacrificial generosity, involvement and partnership, commitment, learning, and leadership) which is/are your strength(s) and passion(s)? Which one(s) needs improvement?

2. Preach, Teach, and Expose Multiplication Values

Brainstorm all of the various ways your church can teach the multiplication values of faith, sacrificial generosity, a kingdom mind-set, involvement, partnership, commitment, learning, and leading. Work these values into everything you do. Also, infuse the following Scriptures references into as many messages as possible: Matthew 18:16; John 12:23–27; John 15:8; Acts 1:8; Acts 13:1–3. Consider using a sermon series, guest speakers, seminars, daily devotionals, testimonies, sermon illustrations, slogans, signs, and songs to drive these values deep into the culture of your congregation.

3. Encourage and Lead Multiplication Values

Once a church can begin to multiply on the micro level, it is much easier to multiply on the macro level. If individuals can share their faith, lead people to Christ, and disciple them (micro multiplication), the church is given a picture of how it could happen on a larger scale by starting a new church (macro multiplication). If a small group can multiply into several groups (micro multiplication), the church is given a picture of how it could happen on a larger scale by starting a new church (macro multiplication).

STEP 3: Influence the Influencers, Inform the Members

"Basic Leadership 101" tells us that people are naturally down on what they are not up on. If people resist change, it is likely related to their need for more information. Whenever you attempt to move a church in a new direction, there are two primary groups that need attention and communication, as defined here.

First: Influence the Influencers

Until the most influential people in your church have bought into the vision, any plan to launch new churches is unlikely to lift off the ground. There are five primary keys/steps to influencing influencers. All five are necessary before going to the rest of the congregation about the details of the plan to plant a daughter church.

1. **Identify the top ten influencers in your church.** These persons are the E. F. Huttons of your church. When they talk, people listen. In a meeting, they are the ones everyone looks to for answers. On Sundays, they are the ones people gather around in the lobby. They may have a title, but not always. They also are likely to have standing in the community, but again, not always. Your top ten members (or "Big Ten") could include staff members, church officers, Sunday school teachers, small group leaders, worship team members, former pastors, or the head of the ladies Bible study. List your "Big Ten" below.

1.

2.

3.

4.

5.

6.

7.

8.

9.

10.

2. Invest in the influencers. People typically buy into the leader before they buy into their vision. You should directly invest in people. If they are the same gender as you, start spending more time with them. If they are the opposite sex, you and your wife should do things with them as couples. You may have several of these types of couples join you in a variety of occasions: to your house for dinner; to your house to watch a big game on television; to attend a concert.

You can also invest in them by ministering to the people they care about the most. This may involve ministering to the couple's teenaged son, visiting their mother in the hospital, or winning their neighbor to Christ. List each of your top ten and one specific way you can invest in them.

1.
2.
3.
4.
5.
6.
7.
8.
9.
10.

3. Individually communicate the vision of church planting according to influencers' passions and experiences. After you have won over the influencers in your church, begin to talk with them about church planting. Individually begin to communicate the vision of becoming a mother church. If one of these individuals loves kids, talk about how the new church will reach more young people. If one of them grew up on the other side of town, share how you hope to plant a new church in that area. If one of them loves evangelism, talk about how many more souls will potentially get saved by launching a new church.

List each of your "Big Ten" and their "hot button" issues.

1.
2.
3.
4.
5.
6.
7.
8.
9.
10.

4. Involve the "Big Ten" in the process. If you leave your "Big Ten" out of the process, church planting will die because it is simply your idea. But if you involve them in the process, they can carry the ball because church planting has also become their idea. Influencers won't own a vision until they participate in carrying it out. Get them involved in the planting of a new church according to their strengths and interests. This may involve asking some of them to study the financial needs of a new church. Others can be asked to prepare Bible studies on church planting, while some can do demographic studies of prime areas. Some members may lead pray meetings specifically aimed at church planting, while some may plan evangelistic efforts. All of your "Big Ten" can help you consider how to sell the vision to the congregation.

List each influencer and how they may participate in the process of planting a new church.

1.
2.
3.
4.
5.
6.
7.

8.

9.

10.

5. Ignite the "Big Ten" to persuade others. Motivate your influencers to be contagious about church planting. Encourage them to invite other couples to their homes for dinner or other gatherings so that they can specifically talk about how they too can help in a church-planting effort.

Second: Inform the Members

Once the influencers are on board with a church-planting project, you can effectively and aggressively inform your members about the specifics of your church's involvement in church planting. Use everything at your disposal—including sermons, banners, slogans, signs, announcements, newsletter articles, and anything else at your disposal—to let them know all of the specifics regarding your church's role in launching new churches.

STEP 4: Determine what type of daughter church planning you will do.

There are several common models of intentional mother-daughter church planting that I would like to highlight. Each model listed here has its own set of strengths and weaknesses. In fact, a given church may use one model in one situation and a different model for a future church-planting effort.

1. The Missionary Model

The example of the missionary model is the church at Antioch, which sent out Barnabas and Paul (see Acts 13:1–3) to plant churches a considerable distance from that city. This is probably the method that was used most frequently from WWII until the turn of the century. In this model, the mother church sends out a planter to launch a new church. For example, when we launched our church in Ohio in 1985, we were sent out by the Lynchburg, Virginia-based Thomas Road Baptist Church with a $546 dollar offering and a prayer.

In 2000 First Baptist Church of Woodstock (Georgia) sent out a team of young couples to Las Vegas to help plant the Hope Baptist Church. Johnnie Hunt, pastor of First Baptist Church, asked Vance Pittman of Memphis to lead the Las Vegas team. Vance was joined by Mike Laughrun, the small groups pastor, and Jeff Riley, the worship pastor, in February 2001 to help start the new church. Seven years later, nearly 2,000 people worship with the church each Sunday. Plus, the church has planted four churches and helped start two others since its founding.

2. Passing the DNA Model

Richard Harris of the North American Mission Board says, "Besides God Himself, the greatest resource for church planting is the mother church."[5] This model involves the mother church giving away members to serve as workers, givers, inviters, and leaders in the new church that will start nearby. The image is that of passing the DNA of the mother church on to the offspring church. The biblical example of this is the large church of Ephesus sending out teams to nearby areas to form at least six other churches (see Rev. 2–3).

Our church in Ohio used this method to plant five new churches in an eight-year period. We would send out a planter and a team of thirty-five to seventy members to serve as the core group for each daughter church project. Our goal was to plant a new church within half an hour drive from the mother church. We also paid the planters' health insurance for three years and took up a large offering to pay for their startup costs. In addition, we also made available to them our office supplies, copiers, and bulk mailing permit. Occasionally we put the planter on our paid church staff for several months prior to the actual launch.

In church planting, just as in physical birth, the larger the birth weight, the bigger the baby. Just as a baby that is born premature with a birth weight of two pounds has a difficult chance at survival and thriving, the same is true of new churches. A church that launches with several hundred people in its first service has a much greater chance of not only surviving, but of growing large and healthy enough so that it later begins to plant churches. We have discovered that the larger the launch team, the larger the attendance for the first public service. And the larger the attendance at the first service, the greater the odds are of success. Therefore, mother churches should send as many people as they can to become a part of the daughter church.

3. The Partner Model

The partner model refers to those occasions when several churches partner together to plant one new church. Each of the participating churches contributes some money, possibly a few people and much prayer. These churches may also send their youth groups to canvas neighborhoods with door-hangers, or a crew to staff the nursery during the new church's first public launch service, or any number of other actions to facilitate the early success of the daughter church.

The strength of this method is that it allows smaller churches to get involved in starting new churches. This is the method that has been largely used by Southern Baptist churches over the years, as they partner with area associations to launch hundreds of new churches each year.

4. The Multisite Model

In this model we see one church meeting for worship in two or more locations under a shared vision, budget, leadership, and board. This is done to continue a momentum and growth that is not limited by the need to keep building new buildings. It also enables a church to fine-tune its ministry to reach diverse elements of the population.

This model has been used by several large churches to start satellite churches, wherein live worship teams are present in alternate locations, while a video of the sermon from the main church is utilized in the satellite churches. Seacoast Church, which calls itself "one church in many locations," wrote the book on this method (*The Multi-site Church Revolution* by Greg Surrat, Greg Ligon, and Warren Bird). At the time of this writing, Seacoast has eighteen nearly *identical* weekend services meeting in nine locations in North and South Carolina. After live worship, a video of Pastor Greg Surrat's sermon is shown live via video feed to the other locations. Each campus has its own pastor and worship leaders. The strength of this model is that it uses the brand, credibility, experience, and resources of the mother church to speed the growth of the daughter churches.

Multisite campuses can also be used to tailor the approach to better reach a specific niche of society. For example, California's Saddleback Church has eight venues each weekend, with each being designed around a different musical style. Styles range from contemporary praise and worship, black gospel, rock and roll, island style, classic hymns, and Spanish. Live musicians lead the worship in the varying venues while a video feed of the Sunday morning message from the main campus is shown in seven of the eight venues.

5. The Single-Site, Multiethnic Model

There are about two hundred people groups that comprise the eighty-five million-plus citizens of the United States. America has obviously become a multicultural, multilanguage nation. Many churches are recognizing this phenomenon and are subsequently planting new ethnic congregations in their buildings. Spanish and Korean are the most popular of these undertakings, while other churches are now hosting congregations that worship in Mandarin, Cantonese, Vietnamese, Russian, and other languages.

STEP 5: Determine the commitment level of your church.

The kingdom of God expands through sacrifice. If you and your church are going to get involved in successful church parenting, you will need to count the cost. Let's examine the seven areas in which your church may pay an additional cost within the frame of a church-planting effort.

1. Time

A successful birth is a nine-month process. After that period, the real parenting begins. Church plants are similar in that they require time spent in finding the church planter, working with the church planter, assisting the church planter, praying for the church planter (as well as the plant), etc.

2. Money

Church plants require money for staff, start-up, facilities, equipment, advertising, printing, etc. You need to determine what costs will be covered by your denomination or association, what part by the church planter, what part by the people who join the church-planting launch team, and what costs will be covered by your church. Realize that there are people who will financially support church-planting projects even though they have not typically given to special offerings in the past.

3. Attention

Launching a new church will draw attention from other activities in which your church is involved or may be contemplating. Consider this factor before you plan for big campaigns or ways to do the launch in conjunction with the campaign.

4. People

You must be willing to send some of your people to join the launch team. Be prepared to send your best people. The launch team should not consist of people I describe as EGRs (Extra Grace Required persons). The launch team should rather consist of people I refer to as MMPs (Most Mission-minded People).

5. Enemy Attack

New churches are more likely to rescue captives from the kingdom of darkness and deliver them into the kingdom of light. The enemy does not like it when his kingdom is plundered. Therefore, as you become involved in church planting, you need to step up the prayer ministries of your church.

6. Prayer

The most important resource you can give a church-planting team is prayer. The team cannot reach its potential apart from concentrated and constant prayer from the sending church.

7. Communication

Whatever of the aforementioned models you use, most problems can be avoided if the doors of communication remain open between the mother church and the church planter. I suggest that you make a simple written commitment that will specifically spell out what is expected in terms of prayer support, financial support, oversight, responsibilities, site selection, equipment, facilities, the launch team, expectations for communication, and the level of connectedness that should be expected between both churches.

Defining Your Church Legacy

Every person and every church is faced with the question of legacy. We all have a driving need to know that our lives have counted for something bigger, deeper, and more lasting, specifically within the framework of the kingdom of God. The knowledge that we are leaving a good legacy infuses life with a wonderful sense of meaning, purpose, personal congruence, and contribution.

My question is this: What legacy will you leave? I want to identify four primary choices that you have.

1. Legacy of Survival

This is the mostly self-centered decision to "get by." Too many churches are merely holding on by solely focusing on paying the bills and limping slowly into heaven. If this defines your legacy, allow me to ask you a question: Did Jesus come to earth, undergo torture, and die so we could merely get by? I believe that we should be willing to cheerfully pay a price in return for all that God has done for us.

2. Legacy of Status Quo

This legacy is the notion of comfortably sticking to a business-as-usual plan. Risk, in this regard, is avoided at all cost. Let me remind you that there is no faith without risk. The only thing for which we ever see Jesus rebuking His disciples was their lack of faith. God is not a God of the status quo. Further, Jesus did not die for the status quo. Read the parable of the talents and see what He said to the man who buried his talent in the ground (see Matt. 25:24–27).

3. Legacy of Success

This is the legacy of measuring success by what we acquire. In individuals, the acquiring of larger houses, better vacations, the accumulation of more "toys," and leaving a big nest egg for our kids is often the measurement of success. But wouldn't a better "nest egg" for future generations be a legacy of faith, sacrifice, and generosity?

For churches, the legacy of success is measured by the three B's: bigger Buildings, larger Budgets and more Bodies in the pews on Sunday mornings. Remember, Jesus was extremely unimpressed with the man who spent his energy greedily building bigger barns for himself (see Luke 12:13–21). Wouldn't it please the Lord more if, instead of merely building bigger churches, we also left the legacy of several healthy daughter churches that were impacting more areas of our communities? Think of the difference it could make if your church parented several new churches over the course of the next several years.

4. Legacy of Significance

A hundred years from now, it won't matter how many things we acquired in this life. The level of our earthly success will be insignificant and forgotten. However, we can have a significant eternal significance in terms of lives we impacted for Christ. If we can lead many to righteousness through church planting, our legacy will shine forever and ever!

I want to close by highlighting a wonderful verse that shows the importance of the legacies we, as Christians, leave behind: "Those who are wise will shine like the bright expanse of the heavens, and those who lead many to righteousness, like the stars forever and ever" (Dan. 12:3).

Notes:

1. *Church Planting Churches*, seminar notebook, DCPI, 5. For many more details about mother-daughter church planting, I highly recommend *The Dynamic Daughter Church Planting Handbook* by Paul Becker and Mark Williams. It is available from DCPI International, 800-255-0431 or www.dcpi.org.

2. Tom Clegg and Warren Bird, *Lost in America: How Your Church Can Impact the World Next Door* (Loveland, CO: Group Publishing, Inc., 2000), 33.

3. Dave Olsen, http://www.theamericanchurch.org.

4. Jerry Falwell, "Falwell's Five Fundamental Facts of Life," TRBC, http://sermons.trbc.org/960804.html.

5. Richard Harris, quoted in *Seven Steps for Planting Churches* (Alpharetta, GA: North American Mission Board, 2004), 1.

APOLOGETICS

CHAPTER 12

Sheep, Goats, and Wolves

Jude Answers Why We Should Do
Apologetics in the Church

by Ergun Caner

I t was a decidedly awkward moment for Pastor Steve.

Upon the recommendation of the director of missions, Steve had invited a guest speaker into his pulpit. The preacher was somewhat known in the community, but Steve did not know him personally. Now the man was preaching in his pulpit, and Steve was cringing on the front pew.

The preacher was passionately making his case that the Bible was trustworthy in matters of faith and practice. With a fervor usually seen only in camp meetings, the man was both preaching and exhorting, and the church members were enthusiastically agreeing with him.

"We believe in Jesus!" he exclaimed.

"Amen!" responded a number of church members.

"We follow Jesus, and not just a book!" he exclaimed.

"Amen!" echoed in the sanctuary.

"And we believe the Bible contains the Word of God!" he concluded.

The people responded again, loudly.

That is what made the moment awkward for Pastor Steve. Not the response from the people, but the reasoning from the pulpit. In a clever twisting of words, this preacher had sounded like a Bible-believing preacher but had presented the classic liberalism of the previous century.

For this guest speaker, the Bible was *not* the complete Word of God; it merely *contained* the Word of God. Steve sat crestfallen on the front pew, pathetically wondering why he had given his pulpit to someone he did not know. How was he going to fix this problem?

The illustration above has taken place countless times in the Christian world. With the subtlety of serpents, deceivers often tear down the gospel from within. Sadly, most church members are not mature enough in the faith to tell the difference. Thus, Christians are led astray from the faith—not by frontal attack, but by clever deception.

As a result, I believe the need for apologetics in the local church has never been greater.

Before the reader begins to lament the ever-worsening condition of the local church, it would be helpful to be reminded that each generation makes the same claim. More than forty years ago, theologian Frank Gaebelein bemoaned this very issue, when he wrote, "One of the major problems of Protestantism today is the biblical illiteracy of the laity."[1]

Without a sound grasp on biblical truth, church members are often led astray by cunning cults, false philosophies, and even outright heresy. The lamentable percentage of members of Christian churches who join cults such as the Latter Day Saints is cause enough for concern.

Sheep, Goats, and Wolves

One pastor shared the following in a meeting last year on the West Coast: "The tragedy is, once I announced my retirement, I began to see warning signs that the transition to the next pastor was not going to be pretty. The deacons brought in a string of guest preachers, and the *funniest* one was invited back. During his interim period, his humor offset a number of teachings he held that were contrary to biblical truth. Still, because he was winsome and easygoing, the people readily accepted him as one of their own. The next thing I knew, he was pastor, and the church never asked him one single doctrinal question!"

What would cause an otherwise normal church to allow such an insult to biblical fidelity? Why would a church filled with deacons, Bible study teachers, and intelligent believers allow for such a swing away from truth? I would like to suggest that it is not overt and conspicuous heresy that leads most churches astray; rather it is *subtle wolves* that typically lead churches astray.

The citation comes from a timely adage that is precisely on point: "There are three types of animals in the church: sheep, goats, and wolves. The job of the shepherd is to love the sheep, convert the goats, and kill the wolves."

Unfortunately, in a culture of expediency, shepherds are often fearful of killing wolves. It is unpopular to speak of doctrine, and unseemly to make such strong decisions as disfellowshiping those who prey upon the flock. Strangely, these days the wolves are often given lead positions on committees in many churches!

We must hasten to add that this is not a slight against contemporary churches, or an issue of style. Churches that worship in styles across the spectrum fall victim to subtle heresies. Neither is this an issue of discipleship, per se. Many churches offer a wide array of classes that take believers into deeper devotion and practice.

This is an issue of discernment and apologetics.

What Is Apologetics?

Apologetics is the biblical practice of defending truth and exposing error. From the Greek term *apologia*, it is found eight times in the New Testament and is often translated as "defense." For example, in Acts 22:1, Paul states, "Brothers and fathers, listen now to my defense [*apologia*] before you." To the church at Corinth, he offers his credentials to criticize the problems in the church, "My defense [*apologia*] to those who examine me . . ." (1 Cor. 9:3). In both cases, the term indicates a carefully stated presentation that answers skeptics and critics.

The apostle Paul saw this as more than just a loud and boisterous shouting session, like activists in the street. He saw the ability to present Christianity to an unbelieving world as a viable calling. In Philippians 1:16, he even goes so far as to state, "I am appointed for the defense [*apologia*] of the gospel." The apostle Paul concurs, and even adds a methodology for apologetics in 1 Peter 3:15: "But sanctify Christ as Lord in your hearts, always being ready to make a defense [*apologia*] to everyone who asks you to give an account for the hope that is in you, yet with gentleness and reverence" (NASB).

I would like to submit four fundamental reasons why churches should teach, train, and prepare our members to defend their faith, even within the walls of the church: (1) the Bible demands it; (2) truth is under attack; (3) young believers are often led away from the faith; and (4) often faithful members are deceived by heresy that sounds true.

Mind and Soul: Because the Bible Demands Intelligent Faith

While our culture emphasizes emotional allegiance, the Bible speaks of a genuine and reasonable faith. We are told, "Do not believe every spirit, but test the spirits to determine if they are from God, because many false prophets have gone out into the world" (1 John 4:1). Further, we are commanded to "test all things. Hold on to what is good" (1 Thess. 5:21).

The mind and heart are linked inexorably in Scripture. The limitations of the flesh—the emotions and feelings that often sway by circumstances—are nowhere seen more clearly than in Paul's words in 2 Corinthians 10:3–5: "For although we are walking in the flesh, we do not wage war in a fleshly way, since the weapons of our warfare are not fleshly, but are powerful through God for the demolition of strongholds. We demolish arguments and every high-minded thing that is raised up against the knowledge of God, taking every thought captive to the obedience of Christ."

The mind of the believer is stronger than the flesh and can withstand the storms of life because it was designed by God to be the filter of truth.

Innovative churches find ways to emphasize this tool of discernment, even through their pulpits. It is not enough to merely exhort believers to act right; they must *believe* right. The truth of Scripture, and the ability to discern between truth and error, is the surest anchor of faith.

Reasonable Faith: Because Christianity Is under Attack

The need for defending the faith in church has never been more required and relevant than now. Today a belief in a personal and intimate God and the truth of Scripture is often viewed as a strange and antiquated link to a superstitious past. Evangelical Christians are openly derided for their belief in Jesus and the Bible. The central premise is clear: it is not enough to simply disciple a Christian devotionally; they must also be discipled intellectually.

In the August 15, 2003, edition of the *New York Times*, the Op-Ed columnist Nicholas D. Kristof mocked our evangelical beliefs. Lamenting the fact that three times as many Americans believe in the virgin birth (83 percent) than do evolution (28 percent), he purported that we believe these things *in spite of* evidence, in a form of mystical and blind faith. In contrast with an unbelieving and skeptical world, Kristof views the fundamentals of our faith as an insult to so-called reasonable thinking.

He even mocks: "The result is a gulf not only between America and the rest of the industrialized world, but a growing split at home as well. One of the most poisonous divides is the one between intellectual and religious America."

His conclusion cannot be more poignant—to men such as Kristof, Christianity is not only unreasonable, it is anti-intellectual.

Losing My Religion: Because Students Leave the Faith

In addition to the need for an intellectual Christian voice in culture, there is added pressure when a Christian student attends a secular university. In 2006 a report was released by two professors from Harvard University and George Mason University. They found the percentage of atheists and agnostics teaching in United States colleges to be 23.4 percent, which is roughly three times greater than in the general population (Electa Draper, the *Denver Post*, 24 September 2007). When our young people leave the home and attend college, they are often unprepared to be confronted with skeptics and critics of Christianity. Though the study shows that some students do become more committed because of intellectual persecution they face, it also notes that for four decades the majority of students have become more apathetic to their beliefs after they enter college.

Some measure of apathy can be blamed on the loosening of the bonds between parent and child during this time. These young people are "spreading their wings," and "leaving the nest," and therefore test the conventions of their youth. And while some simply stop attending church, others are lured away by skeptics and cynics. Often authority figures such as professors, scholars, and speakers attack their faith. Without a foundation of apologetics, these students begin to question their faith. This is not because of our training, but precisely due to the lack of training we provide.

Without an apologetic training for our youth, the students do not anticipate the attacks on their faith.

Wandering Sheep: Because Members Get Divorced

Finally, the lack of apologetics in our churches results in losing members, both to cults that teach a false form of Christianity or to other world religions. When we neglect to train our people in doctrine and truth, we leave them susceptible to the wiles of groups that deny Christ as Lord and Savior. Even the cults recognize our weakness in this regard. Elder John Taylor, an ordained "Apostle" in the Latter Day Saints (Mormons) and personal friend of Joseph Smith, made this observation during his Tabernacle address on May 6, 1870: "Christianity, at the present time, is no more enlightened than other systems have been. What does the Christian world know about God? Nothing . . . why so far as the things of God are concerned, they are the veriest fools; they know neither God nor the things of God" (*Journal of Discourses* 13:225).

The Agony of Apologetics (Jude 1–3)

In offering churches a rationale for apologetic training, I often use the book of Jude as a prime foundation. The descriptions and reasoning in this brief epistle are so vivid and clear, even the most sentimental Christian must agree that truth is the highest importance in faith. Faith in faith is not important. The object of faith is the most pertinent issue.

The book of Jude is not addressed to a specific church or congregation. Unlike the other named books in the New Testament, Jude simply writes "to those who are the called, loved by God the Father and kept by Jesus Christ" (v. 1). The universal nature of his writing, however, is immediately evident. God has inspired Jude to write to every Christian who is "called . . . loved . . . and kept."

The immediate purpose of the book is also universal. Jude emphatically states that he "found it necessary to write and exhort you to contend for the faith that was delivered to the saints once for all" (v. 3). The English word "contend" is taken from the Greek word *epagonizomai*, which means "to fight earnestly," or "fight with all one's heart." The gospel message has been passed down as a type of spiritual birthright, and Jude states we must valiantly defend it. The term is actually a preposition (*epi*) attached to the word from which we get our term *agony*. We are called to "agonize against" those who would attempt to take away the gospel message.

The nature of this struggle is still yet to be determined thus far in the letter, but the subject to whom Jude is writing is clear: it is *all believers*! Since all believers fall into the category of the "called . . . loved by God and kept by Jesus Christ," then his admonition is to "contend." As distasteful as this may be for some believers, defending the faith is central to being a believer in Christ.

The Nature of Wolves and the Reason for Apologetics (Jude 4)

"For certain men, who were designated for this judgment long ago, have come in by stealth; they are ungodly, turning the grace of our God into promiscuity and denying our only Master and Lord, Jesus Christ" (Jude 4).

Jude answers the immediate and logical question, why fight? He notes that certain people have crept into the church. The word *pareisduno* means to sneak in secretly, so as to not be discovered. He immediately discloses the nature of these subtle invaders. They are ungodly, and the term *promiscuity* is better translated "unbridled lust" or "unleashed carnage." In denying the grace of Christ, they are substituting their own passions with demonic fervor.

The message preached by these trespassers is shown in stark contrast in just a brief sentence: Jude states what they stand for and what they stand against. They stand *against* the Lordship of Jesus Christ. They stand *in favor of* their own sensual desires. The most shocking element of the verse is their location: they have crept into the fellowship. These persons are worse than storms outside of the church. They are now like termites that now threaten the very foundation of the fellowship.

As a young Christian, I became aware of such people when my pastor stood against a teacher in the church and removed him publicly from his position. The man had begun to teach a form of idolatry, advocating that a believer could become perfect and sinless, if only they would follow his teachings. Though we are called to be holy as He is holy (see Lev. 19:2), the achievement of perfection is only found in heaven. However, the subtlety of his argument was so insidious that students in his class began to follow him almost blindly. His words sounded correct and he used Scripture to allegedly back his claims. His teaching, however, was woefully heretical. Only Christ was perfect on the earth.

Our pastor rose one Sunday and noted that, along with the deacons, he had taken steps to bring the man back to biblical truth. The arrogance with which the man responded and his stubborn adherence to this teaching of sinlessness brought the issue before the church. Otherwise godly men and women—many of whom had been in the church for many years—followed that man out of the church that morning.

The Longevity of Wolves: They Have Always Been with Us (Jude 5–7)

As a relatively new believer, I was perplexed. How could people who had been Christians for so long be so easily fooled by such a teacher? Jude anticipates this question in the next three verses. He offers three biblical examples of the deception of those who should have known better.

In Egypt: First, Jude offers the example of those who had followed God out of the slavery of Egypt. While they had seen the provision of God daily in provision, they still did not believe, and because of it, "the Lord, having first of all saved a people out of Egypt, later destroyed those who did not believe" (v. 5).

In Heaven: Shockingly, Jude offers a stark reminder of willful ignorance by citing the fall of the angels who followed Satan. Referring to Isaiah 14 and Ezekiel 28, Jude writes, "He has kept, with eternal chains in darkness for the judgment of the great day, angels who did not keep their own position but deserted their proper dwelling" (v. 6).

In Sodom and Gomorrah: Third, Jude shows that entire cities have been deceived. He writes, "In the same way, Sodom and Gomorrah and the cities around them committed sexual immorality and practiced perversions, just as they did, and serve as an example by undergoing the punishment of eternal fire" (v. 7).

What becomes readily apparent in these illustrations is the danger of influence. By our silence, we will allow these ungodly people to lead our people astray. The children of Israel had seen God as a pillar of smoke and fire and had followed. The angels were literally around the throne of God! Yet, even close proximity to God was not enough insurance to prevent them from following a lie.

The Character of Wolves: Unreasoning Animals (Jude 8–16)

Jude begins to disclose the characteristics of these false leaders, intimating the reason why people follow them. In verse 8, he writes, "Nevertheless, these dreamers likewise defile their flesh, despise authority, and blaspheme glorious beings." In comparing them to Satan's desire to fight over the body of Moses, he adds, "But these people blaspheme anything they don't understand, and what they know by instinct, like unreasoning animals—they destroy themselves with these things."

Clearly these sinister teachers are compelled by the flesh and appeal to the flesh. Either through pride or lust, they are driven to pull away as many people as they possibly can. A cursory reading of the news shows this to be true. People willingly follow lies that even the most intelligent person would reject, purely because of the winsome nature of the leader.

Marshall Applewhite told the "Heaven's Gate" followers that the comet would take them home, if only they would commit suicide. Amazingly thirty-eight people followed him in 1997. Tom Cruise becomes the spokesman for Scientology, and their recruiting numbers double. Even when the end result is death or personal poverty, the flesh draws followers.

After giving three more Old Testament examples of their impeding destruction, Jude then describes their nature in more poignant language. He states, "These are the ones who are like dangerous reefs at your love feasts. They feast with you, nurturing only themselves without fear. They are waterless clouds carried along by winds; trees in late autumn—fruitless, twice dead, pulled out by the roots; wild waves of the sea, foaming up their shameful deeds; wandering stars for whom is reserved the blackness of darkness forever!" (Jude 12–13).

The word "reefs" is *spilas* in the Greek. It is a metaphor for the jagged rocks, hidden beneath the surf that can implode and sink ships. The implication is that they are more than just worthless; they are *dangerous*. They have no foundation (roots), but they do have an effect—they can sink other believers.

Finally, in verse 16, he lays them bare by detailing their most menacing characteristic: their hypocrisy. He writes, "These people are discontented grumblers, walking according to their desires; their mouths utter arrogant words, flattering people for their own advantage." The purpose of the deceiver is to draw men unto himself. He does not care about the heart and pain of the follower; he cares only for his own desires.

Winning the War with Wolves (Jude 17–25)

The purpose of the apologist is emphasized immediately. In order to win a victory against the sinister and sensual, we must first present a godly example of true faith, and then provide a godly escape for those who may fall under their spell. Before an apologist can be an effective witness, he or she must first be prepared. This augurs one of the most essential truths in apologetics: we do not set out to win arguments; we set out to win souls.

Jude begins: "But you, dear friends, remember the words foretold by the apostles of our Lord Jesus Christ; they told you, 'In the end time there will be scoffers walking according to their own ungodly desires.' These people create divisions and are merely natural, not having the Spirit. But you, dear friends, building yourselves up in your most holy faith and praying in the Holy Spirit, keep yourselves in the love of God, expecting the mercy of our Lord Jesus Christ for eternal life" (Jude 17–21).

Before I can enter battle, I must be protected by the armor of God. Being built up in the most holy faith guards my own heart. Praying in the Holy Spirit offers me the preparation I need. Jude echoes the words of our Lord in Luke 12:12: "For the Holy Spirit will teach you at that very hour what must be said." Being kept in the love of God measures my motives, and the expectation of mercy keeps my perspective.

This is offered in stark contrast to those who are the wolves. They operate by divisions and personal gain. Clearly here God promises that we have a Holy Weapon that renders them powerless—the Holy Spirit. Though they scoff, they cannot stand against His divine enablement.

Jude then offers us the threefold battle plan stated at the beginning of this chapter. "Have mercy on some who doubt; save others by snatching them from the fire; on others have mercy in fear, hating even the garment defiled by the flesh" (Jude 22–23).

Look at the text again, and consider the sheep, goats, and wolves. We are to have mercy on those who may consider the deception (sheep). The word for mercy is *eleeo*, and it connotes bringing much-needed aid. We are to rescue those who are sympathetic to their teachings (goats). Finally, we are to even have mercy with fear on those who have brought this evil to us (wolves).

Consider that final admonition for a moment. We do not capriciously destroy people, kick them out of our churches, mock their teachings, or rejoice at their destruction! The leaders of these false religions and cults are people for whom Christ died (see 2 Pet. 3:9). The fundamental principle of apologetics is our concern here yet again. We must be careful to excise the heresy but always pray for their salvation. Even though we hate their sin and hate their teaching, we do not hate them. Our actions to protect the flock must be swift and clear. We can never allow our people to be vulnerable to heresy and false philosophies. However, we must continue to pray for their salvation.

The word "fear" used in verse 23 is the Greek word from which we get the English term *phobia*. It is a reminder that every person, without proper training and apologetic discipleship, is susceptible to these errors. Perhaps that is the reason Jude concludes his letter with the following: "Now to Him who is able to *protect you from stumbling* and to make you stand in the presence of His glory, blameless and with great joy, to the only God our Savior, through Jesus Christ our Lord, be glory, majesty, power, and authority before all time, now, and forever" (Jude 24–25, emphasis added).

God is able to keep you from stumbling. *God is able* to make you stand blameless and with great joy. Jude is not suggesting that a believer can lose his salvation, but he does offer us a clear path to avoid becoming a prodigal, miserable and off the path of God's perfect will. We can avoid following wolves who attempt to lead us astray, and innovative evangelical churches can become apologetic training centers that keep others from doing so, as well.

Notes

1. "Perspective on American Christianity," *Christianity Today*, 23 April 1965, 785).

CHAPTER 13

What Is Worth Defending in the Postmodern Culture?

by Ed Hindson

Apologetics involves the art of persuasion and the defense of the Christian faith. The concept is derived from the Greek *apologia*, meaning, "to give an answer." The Bible itself urges us to "make a defense to everyone who asks you to give an account for the hope that is in you" (1 Pet. 3:15 NASB). While it is necessary for the Holy Spirit to illuminate our minds to God's truth, He does so by appealing to both the sacred text and to human reasoning. Thus, faith and reason are allies in the quest for truth.

In classical Christian orthodoxy, faith precedes reason, but it certainly does not eliminate it. Christianity is not a mindless religion of mystical experiences that are devoid of reasonable conclusions. To the contrary, Christianity is the most well-reasoned, factually-based religion on the planet. Over the centuries God has raised up great minds to defend the legitimacy of the Christian faith.

The church has withstood the attacks of everything from Gnosticism to liberalism. But today we face a new challenge—the irrepressible cynicism of postmodernism. Michael Horton has observed: "The modern era has come to an end, and the post-modern self is now in the ascendancy."[1] As a result, some churches are repackaging their message to appeal to the postmodern mind, in which experience replaces reason. Their approach basically says: "Let's enjoy our religion, even if we can't explain it!" As a result, basic biblical doctrines are avoided, neglected, and, in some cases, even dismissed as irrelevant.

Today's church is at a great crossroads in the history of Christianity. Which way we go will determine the shape of the church in the future. It has often been observed that ministry styles (worship, music, preaching) may change but the message should remain the same. So the questions we are facing are simply: What is that message? And what are the essential truths of Christianity that are worth defending?

Inspiration of Scripture

The Christian faith is based upon the Bible. Our understanding of God, Christ, and salvation is based upon the revelation of truth in the Word of God. The Bible itself claims: "All Scripture is inspired by God and is profitable for teaching, for rebuking, for correcting, for training in righteousness, so that the man of God may be complete, equipped for every good work" (2 Tim. 3:16–17).

Charles Ryrie defines inspiration as God moving the human authors of the Bible to compose and record this message without error in their own words.[2] Without an inerrant Bible, we have no assurance of the credibility of any of our statements about God and His work in our lives. When Jesus Himself was confronted by Satan, He responded by quoting the Scripture and stating: "It is written: Man must not live on bread alone but on every word that comes from the mouth of God" (Matt. 4:4).

Notice Jesus' emphasis on "every word" from God. His own use of Scripture during His earthly ministry indicates that He had total confidence in the inspiration of all the Scripture. Jesus even rebuked some of the religious leaders of His day, saying: "You are deceived, because you don't know the Scriptures or the power of God" (Matt. 22:29). For Jesus, the inspiration of the Bible was itself a demonstration of the power of God.

It is one thing to believe in and defend the inspiration of Scripture. It is another matter altogether to read it, understand it, and internalize its truths. The inspired text can only affect our daily lives as we study it and apply it. Believing it to be inspired alone will not change how we live without our searching its truths to impact our lives. Real Christianity must be rooted in biblical truth and lived in the reality of life's challenges. Therefore, the Bible speaks to issues of marriage, family, community, relationships, and practical living. It speaks with the same authority as it does in telling us how to get through life as it does in telling us how to get to heaven.

Existence of God

People living in primitive cultures almost always believe in God. They don't seem to wrestle intellectually with the issue of the existence of God. To them God's existence is self evident. Their only questions are: Who is He and how can I know Him? However, that is not the case with the postmodern generation. They not only question the existence of God but seem to want to put Him on trial. Horton observes that "the MTV generation appears to be reacting against evangelical sentimentality with a vengeance."[3]

Understanding God has always been a challenge to the human mind. How can God be sovereign, yet allow human freedom? How can He be good, yet allow evil to exist? How can He love sinners, yet judge their sin? On the one hand we believe that we can know God personally, yet on the other hand He is incomprehensible in that we cannot fully comprehend all that He is. Despite our human limitations, the Bible clearly tells us that we fallible beings can know the infallible God.

Hebrews 11:6 puts it like this: "Now without faith it is impossible to please God, for the one who draws near to Him must believe that He exists and rewards those who seek Him." If God really exists, He is the only source of our knowledge about Him. God has revealed Himself to us in Scripture. In doing so, He has revealed many things about Himself: His eternality, holiness, justice, love, grace, goodness, and righteousness.

As we read about the God of the Bible, we come to know who He is and how He relates to us personally. Ryrie expresses it this way: "Our knowledge about God should deepen our relationship with Him, which in turn increases our desire to know more about Him."[4] The very fact that God can be known by faith is the basis of the biblical message. Thus, Jesus said: "Love the Lord your God with all your heart, with all your soul, and with all your mind" (Matt. 22:37). The prophet Jeremiah expresses God's heart when he writes: "You will call to Me and . . . you will seek Me and find Me when you search for Me with all your heart" (Jer. 29:12–13).

Deity of Christ

It is one thing to believe in the existence of God; it is another matter altogether to believe that Jesus Christ was God in the flesh. It is common today to hear liberal theologians on television specials state that Jesus was a great teacher but that He never really claimed to be God. Of course, such remarks run contrary to everything Jesus said about Himself.

Jesus claimed to have come from heaven, to be equal with God, to be the very incarnation of God, and to represent the power and authority of God. There can be no doubt that He believed He was God. That very claim brought charges of blasphemy, cries of anger, attempts at stoning and finally, the crucifixion itself.

Notice what Jesus said about Himself:

"I am He" (the Messiah). (John 4:26)

"[These are] the Scriptures [that] testify about Me." (John 5:39)

"Before Abraham was born, I am!" (John 8:58 NIV)

"I and the Father are one." (John 10:30 NIV)

"Anyone who has seen me has seen the Father." (John 14:9 NIV)

It is one thing to claim to be God; it is another to demonstrate it. Jesus healed the sick, raised the dead, walked on water, calmed the storm, and fed the multitudes. He made the blind see, the lame walk, and claimed to have the authority to forgive our sins. What did others think of Him? They too were convinced that He was God. Look at what they said about Him:

> *John the Baptist*: "Here is the Lamb of God, who takes away the sin of the world" (John 1:29).
>
> *Simon Peter*: "You are the Messiah, the Son of the living God!" (Matt. 16:16).
>
> *Nathaniel*: "Rabbi, . . . You are the Son of God! You are the King of Israel!" (John 1:49).
>
> *The Samaritans*: "We know that this man really is the Savior of the world" (John 4:42 NIV).
>
> *The Jews*: "He was even calling God His own Father, making Himself equal with God" (John 5:18).
>
> *The disciples*: "Truly You are the Son of God!" (Matt. 14:33).
>
> *Martha*: "Yes, Lord . . . I believe You are the Messiah, the Son of God" (John 11:27).
>
> *Roman centurion*: "This man really was God's Son!" (Matt. 27:54).
>
> *Thomas*: "My Lord and my God!" (John 20:28).

After you evaluate all the evidence for yourself, you too must ask, "Who is Jesus Christ? Liar? Lunatic? Or Lord?" C. S. Lewis said: "You can shut Him up for a fool; you can spit at Him and kill Him as a demon; or you can fall at His feet and call Him Lord and God."[5]

Supremacy of Christ

If Jesus Christ is really God in the flesh, we must worship Him and acknowledge His supremacy as Lord of our lives. The apostle Paul understood this when he wrote: "For this reason God also highly exalted Him and gave Him the name that is above every name, so that at the name of Jesus every knee should bow—of those who are in heaven . . .—and every tongue should confess that Jesus Christ is Lord, to the glory of God the Father" (Phil. 2:9–11).

John the Revelator expresses this same spirit of exaltation as he describes the scene in heaven: "Then I looked, and I heard the voice of many angels around the throne and the living creatures and the elders; and the number of them was myriads of myriads, and thousands of thousands, saying with a loud voice, 'Worthy is the Lamb that was slain to receive power and riches and wisdom and might and honor and glory and blessing'" (Rev. 5:11–12 NASB).

If the biblical writers acknowledged the exaltation and supremacy of Christ, how much more should we? It is one thing to affirm His deity. It is another to live, serve, and worship as though He is divine. No wonder, Paul said of Jesus, "That He might come to have first place in everything" (Col. 1:18).

This is the basis of true Christian worship. We live to bring glory to God and to exalt the risen Savior with our praise, worship, and service. He is our all in all. The Christian life is really not about us. It is all about Him! The church that wins the lost, captivates the soul, challenges the mind, and makes true disciples is the church that exalts the Savior. When He is on display, all kinds of people are drawn to Him.

Gospel of Salvation

Jesus made it clear that He came to seek and save the lost. He is the epitome of divine love, sufficient grace, and eternal hope. No one loves the lost like He does. That love took Him to the cross to die for your sins (see 1 Cor. 15:1–4). The good news of the gospel compels us to believe that He died for us personally. Therefore He calls upon us to trust His death as a sufficient payment for our sins.

Faith is the act of believing that activates our commitment to Jesus Christ as our personal Savior. It is the key that personalizes our relationship to Him. Saving faith means that we believe Jesus died for our sins and that He offers us forgiveness and eternal life. Our act of faith receives the free gift of salvation, believes God's offer of grace to be sincere and trusts Him to keep His promises—forever.

Charles Spurgeon said it best a century ago when he wrote: "You may study, look and meditate, but Jesus is a greater Savior than you think Him to be even when your thoughts are at their highest."[6] Jesus is more willing to save us than we are willing to ask. But once we do ask, He does all the rest. No wonder they call Him the Savior!

Jesus came so that we might know God personally. He suffered and died for our sins so that they might be paid in full (see 1 Pet. 2:21–24). Then He rose from the dead to offer us the gift of eternal life (see John 10:28). We receive that gift by faith. Believing in Jesus is an act of trust by which we affirm that what He did on the cross is enough to save us, transform us, and assure our eternal destiny. Therefore, the Bible promises: "Everyone who calls on the name of the Lord will be saved" (Rom. 10:13).

Reality of the Resurrection

The resurrection is the ultimate proof that Jesus is the Son of God. It is the strongest argument for the truth of Christianity.

It separates Jesus from all other religious leaders. He is not just a great teacher; He is a risen Savior!

The resurrection of Jesus Christ is the most unique event in all the world. There is nothing else to compare to it. First, He is the only person to raise Himself from the dead. Second, He is the only person ever raised who did not later die a natural death. In fact, His resurrection is proof that He does indeed have the power to raise us to life.

Critics of the Christian gospel are hard-pressed to discount the resurrection story. There were so many eyewitnesses. Every one of the disciples eventually sealed his testimony with his life. Each one died a martyr, claiming the message was true.

Then there are all the personal aspects of the story. The despair of the disciples. The confusion among the women who found the stone rolled away. The panic of the Jewish leaders. The embarrassment of the Roman officials. The assertion by Thomas that the others were deceived.

Who could blame Thomas? The resurrection sounded too good to be true. Perhaps the disciples just *thought* they saw Him. But, there was that part about touching Him and watching Him eat. And the Bible study around the table. One week later Jesus appeared to all the disciples, Thomas included. The doors were locked, the disciples were assembled, and Jesus appeared instantly in the room. He turned to Thomas. He looked right at him, held out His nail-scarred hand, and said, "Put your finger here and observe My hands. Reach out your hand and put it into My side" (John 20:27).

Thomas was totally overcome. He fell at Jesus' feet and cried, "My Lord and my God!" There was no doubting this time. He knew Jesus was alive. He had seen Him for himself! "Because you have seen Me, you have believed," Jesus said. "Those who believe without seeing are blessed" (John 20:29).

That's where we come in. We have not actually seen the risen Christ, even though ours is a faith based upon facts. Those facts are clearly expressed in the Gospel accounts and were so convincing that thousands of people living at the time came to believe them and to pass them on to us.

We, too, must consider those facts. Someone rolled away the stone. The body was missing, and no one ever produced it to counter the claims of the resurrection. The disciples, hundreds of them, claimed to have seen the risen Christ (see 1 Cor. 15:6). Most of them were still living when the apostles were evangelizing the world, writing the Gospels, and distributing their epistles. Anyone could certainly have checked out the story for themselves.

If the people who lived closest to the event believed it, how much more should we believe it! Time has not invalidated their testimony; it has only reinforced its truth. If Jesus really rose from the dead, He is the greatest person who ever lived. If He is actually alive today, He is a living Savior. He, and He alone, can grant eternal life, because He, and He alone, is the author of life. "I am the resurrection and the life," He said. "The one who believes in Me, even if he dies will live" (John 11:25). What a claim! There is no greater promise. And there is no greater person.

Power of the Spirit

Jesus prepared the disciples for His eventual departure into heaven by promising to send "another counselor to be with you forever. He is the Spirit of truth" (John 14:16–17). From the very beginning of Jesus' ministry, John the Baptist had declared: "He is the One who baptizes with the Holy Spirit" (John 1:33). The work of Christ is carried on today by the ministry of the Holy Spirit. Any church that hopes to make an impact on today's world must be empowered by the Spirit.

When Jesus ascended into heaven, He promised the disciples, "But you will receive power when the Holy Spirit has come upon you, and you will be My witnesses in Jerusalem, in all Judea and Samaria, and to the ends of the earth" (Acts 1:8). Beginning on the Day of Pentecost, the Holy Spirit descended, baptizing believers into the body of Christ—the New Testament church.

The Holy Spirit is distinct from the Father and the Son, yet He exists together with them in one essence of indivisible unity. He is nothing less than God Himself. He is coequal and coeternal with the Father and the Son. His ministry is to call our attention, not to Himself, but to the Son. Jesus said, "He will glorify Me, because He will take from what is Mine and declare it to you" (John 16:14). Therefore, we know that the Spirit-empowered church is one that exalts the Savior.

The work of the Holy Spirit involves several aspects that affect the life of the believer. First, the Holy Spirit ignites the believer with *spiritual life*. Jesus referred to this experience as being "born of the Spirit" (John 3:6–8). He describes this event as being "born again" (John 3:3). Peter refers to this experience as being "made alive by the Spirit" (1 Pet. 3:18 NIV) and being "born again . . . through the . . . word of God" (1 Pet. 1:23).

The new birth occurs when we receive Christ by faith. The Holy Spirit convicts us of our sin, convinces us of our need for the Savior, and invites us to believe in Him. At that moment we are reborn by the power of the Holy Spirit. The Bible describes this experience as passing from death to life (see John 5:24). The apostle Paul put it this way: "The wages of sin is death, but the gift of God is eternal life in Christ Jesus our Lord" (Rom. 6:23).

Second, the Holy Spirit *baptizes* us into the body of Christ. First Corinthians 12:13 tells us: "For we were all baptized by one Spirit into one body—whether Jews or Greeks, whether slaves or free—and we were all made to drink of one Spirit." While Christians differ on how to explain the baptism of the Spirit, this passage seems to clearly state that once the transition period in the book of Acts was complete, the baptism of the Spirit was normative for all believers.

Third, the Spirit *seals* us to Christ. This process is explained in Ephesians 1:13, which says: "In Him you also trusted, after you heard the word of truth, the gospel of your salvation; in whom also, having believed, you were sealed with the Holy Spirit of promise" (NKJV). The next verse explains that the sealing of the Spirit guarantees our eternal inheritance. In other words, once we believe, we are born again, baptized, and sealed by the Holy Spirit. From that point on, our spiritual life is eternally transformed.

Fourth, the Holy Spirit *indwells* the believer. Romans 8:9 explains this experience as the Spirit of God dwelling in us. The passage goes on to say, "But if anyone does not have the Spirit of Christ, he does not belong to Him." Thus, the indwelling of the Spirit indicates that the believer has been born of the Spirit and the Spirit dwells (or lives) in him or her. Thus, the Christian life is one of living in the Spirit, not simply one of self-discipline and determination. We live differently because we are different—the Holy Spirit lives in us.

Finally, there is the *filling* of the Holy Spirit, which may be repeated often in the believer's life. Unlike the other aspects of the Spirit's work, the filling is not permanent. Thus, we are commanded to "be filled with the Spirit" (Eph. 5:18). This same term is used of Stephen (see Acts 7:55), Barnabas (see Acts 11:24), and the disciples (see Acts 13:52). Each was filled with the Spirit. In Galatians 5:15–18, Paul urges us to "walk by the Spirit" and to be "led by the Spirit." This results in our producing the "fruit of the Spirit" (Gal. 5:22–23).

However we define the distinctions of the Spirit's work and ministry, one thing is obvious—we can't function without the Holy Spirit. He alone ignites our spiritually dead hearts and makes us alive in Christ. He baptizes us into the body of Christ, seals us to Christ, and indwells us permanently so that we can live for Christ. Then He fills us repeatedly for service to Christ. Therefore, the church that really makes a difference in people's lives must be a Spirit-filled church that is alive and vibrant with the glory of God.

Importance of the Church

The true church of Jesus Christ is not a man-made institution. While many postmoderns claim to love Jesus, they readily admit a dislike or even distrust of the institutional church. In light of the human failures of pastors and priests and the abuses of some extremist ministries—who can blame them? Yet, some churches continue to grow and flourish. What is it that still attracts millions of churchgoers every week?

First, we need to remember that the church was Jesus' idea. He announced it, predicted its success, and promised its perpetuity. Facing His impending rejection by His own people, Jesus took His disciples to the remote Gentile region of Caesarea Philippi. There, He announced: "I will build My church, and the forces of Hades will not overpower it" (Matt. 16:18).

The phrase, "I will build" contains an action verb with continuing effect. It means: "I will continue to build." Jesus predicted the ultimate growth of the church by the spread of the gospel. Having given the *Great Prediction* (building the church), He then gave the *Great Commission* to "go, therefore, and make disciples of all nations" (Matt. 28:19). From the very beginning—at Pentecost until this present day—that is exactly what Christian believers have done. They have often risked their lives to take the "good news" of the gospel to the furthest regions of the planet. Those who have taken the Great Commission the most seriously have done the most to spread the gospel, win the lost, plant churches, and disciple believers.

Jesus Himself promised to perpetuate the church, reminding us: "I am with you always, to the end of the age" (Matt. 28:20). He made it clear that He would continue to bless the true church, which proclaims His message unashamedly to the entire world. God has not abandoned the church. He has not given up on it nor changed His plan for the present age. While some institutional churches may fail and their light may burn out, that does not mean that the Lord of the church has abandoned the church.

The apostle Paul foresaw the day when Christ would return for the church and call her home to heaven in the rapture. He referred to those who would be "still alive at the Lord's coming" (1 Thess. 4:15). This passage makes it clear that there will still be true believers on the earth at the end of the age when Jesus returns to take us home to the Father's house (see John 14:1–4).

Jesus loves the church and refers to her as a bride and Himself as the Bridegroom (see Matt. 25:1–13). The apostle Paul emphasizes this same theme in Ephesians 5:25–33, where he instructs husbands to love their wives "just as also Christ loved the church and gave Himself for her" (v. 25). Revelation 19:7–10 describes the spiritual marriage of Christ (the Lamb) to the bride (the church) in heaven. These verses would be irrelevant if Jesus ever intended to abandon the church. People may give up on certain man-made forms of the church, but Christ will never abandon the true church. If He loves the church, then so should we.

Theologians have long recognized the distinction between the *universal* church, composed of all believers of all time since Pentecost, and the *visible* church on earth, made up of baptized professing believers at any given time in the history of the church. Commenting on this distinction, Christian apologist Norman Geisler says: "In relation to the universal church, the purpose of the local church is to be a visible manifestation, an outward expression of the inward character of Christ's body, manifesting its recognition of His headship and our unity."[7]

When we do church right, God blesses it. Things happen in the spiritual realm that cannot be explained by mere human effort. When God is at work through the power of His Spirit, Christ Himself will build the church. Thus, our theme is "Not I, but Christ." He must be worshiped, glorified, honored, and praised. His gospel must be clearly proclaimed, "for there is no other name under heaven given to people by which we must be saved" (Acts 4:12).

Hope of Christ's Return

When Jesus met with the disciples on the night before He went to the cross, He made a wonderful promise: "I am going away to prepare a place for you. If I go away and prepare a place for you, I will come back and receive you to Myself, so that where I am you may be also" (John 14:2–3). Jesus spoke these words to the eleven believing disciples, Judas having already left the room. This was the first indication that Jesus would return one day for His own.

The second coming of Christ is mentioned more than three hundred times in the New Testament, making it one of the most prominent doctrines in all the Bible. Christ's first coming to earth can be separated into several parts: His birth, ministry, death, resurrection, and ascension. Likewise, the Second Coming also has several aspects: the rapture of the church, the tribulation on earth, the literal return of Christ, the millennial kingdom, and the eternal state. These are each specific dimensions of His Second Coming. They do not involve multiple comings.

Jesus is only coming once to take the believers home to heaven. Paul explains it like this: "For the Lord Himself will descend from heaven with a shout, with the archangel's voice, and with the trumpet of God, and the dead in Christ will rise first. Then we who are still alive will be caught up together with them in the clouds to meet the Lord in the air; and so we will always be with the Lord" (1 Thess. 4:16–17).

We may debate *when* and *how* this rapture (Greek, *harpazo*, "to snatch" or "catch away") will occur, but what is very obvious is that it *will* occur! There must be a time when Jesus returns in the clouds to rapture His bride, the church, home to heaven to the marriage described in Revelation 19:7–9. At some point in time, the church must be taken to the marriage in heaven *before* she returns with Christ to reign with Him on earth (see 19:8, 14).

We believe the rapture could occur at any moment and that it will occur *before* the time of tribulation. That is why Jesus told us to "be alert" and to "be ready" for Him to come (see Matt. 24:42, 44). This admonition would be meaningless if the tribulation and the rise of the Antichrist were to come first. Therefore, we are not watching for the Antichrist to come. We are watching for Jesus Christ to come! In 1 Corinthians 15:51–57, Paul explains that "we will not all fall asleep [die], but we will all be changed, in a moment, in the twinkling of an eye, at the last trumpet. For the trumpet will sound, and the dead will be raised incorruptible, and we [the living] will be changed." No wonder, Paul called this event the "blessed hope" (Titus 2:13).

In the rapture, Christ returns *for* His own, but in the glorious appearing, He returns *with* His own. Having taken the bride (the church) home to heaven to the marriage (see Rev. 19:7–9), He then returns to earth with the bride at His side (see Rev. 19:14) robed in white from the wedding ceremony. This aspect of His Second Coming results in His triumph at Armageddon (see Rev. 16:16), when the beast and the false prophet are cast alive into the lake of fire (see Rev. 19:20) and Satan is bound in the abyss for a thousand years (see Rev. 20:1–3). This has never yet happened in history. These events will only be fulfilled when Jesus returns to earth.

While Christian believers may differ on how they interpret these events, we dare not lose sight of the fact that Jesus is coming again. The church that lives with the Second Coming in view has always been the most committed to holy living, evangelism, missions, and social justice. Those who have been the most heavenly-minded have actually done the most earthly good.

Assurance of Heaven

Ultimately the Bible tells us how to go to heaven. It also tells us how to live life on earth. In the meantime, we are called of God to make a difference in the world in which we live. Our very lives are to be the "salt of the earth" and the "light of the world" (Matt. 5:13–16). But in the end, Scripture reminds us that heaven is our real destiny.

In this day of affluence and material prosperity, it is easy for us to forget that heaven is our real home. Many Christians are so preoccupied with earthly pleasures that they would be very satisfied if heaven would simply wait. For some today, heaven is only a topic of minor interest instead of our major objective.

We must remember, however, that this world is no friend to grace. As time passes, we should expect a continual moral decline in secular society. The Bible reminds us that there will be an "increase of wickedness" and that "terrible times" will come in the last days (Matt. 24:12; 2 Tim. 3:1 NIV). In the meantime, whatever success we have in this world must be measured in the light of our eternal destiny. If we make heaven our primary point of reference, it will transform our relationship to everything that is temporary in this world.

Jesus promised to give eternal life to all who would believe in Him (see John 5:24). It was the hope of this promise that ignited the hearts of the early Christians to take that to the world. "Believe on the Lord Jesus Christ, and you will be saved," Paul told the Philippians jailor (see Acts 16:31).

Jesus made it clear that one's eternal destiny is the result of his or her own decision. In light of the biblical claim that Jesus is the only way to heaven (see John 14:6), we must ask ourselves: Is He telling the truth? Is Jesus Who He claimed to be? Can I trust His promises? Dare I put my hope of eternity in Him? Can He really save me and take me home to heaven? Only you and I can answer those questions, but answer them we must.

The Bible assures us that we have in Jesus Christ a great High Priest who has gone before us into heaven and invites us to "approach the throne of grace with boldness, so that we may receive mercy and find grace to help us at the proper time" (Heb. 4:16). No one loves you like Jesus loves you. He alone died for your sins and He alone can give you eternal life and the hope of heaven.

There are many other concepts that are part of the ministry of the church, but these ten are essential if we are to tell the truth to our generation. These are the essentials of the faith that every generation of believers must defend and thereby "contend for the faith that was delivered to the saints once for all" (Jude 3).

Notes

1. Michael Horton, *We Believe* (Nashville: Word Publishing, 1998), 1.

2. Charles Ryrie, *Basic Theology* (Wheaton, IL: Victor Books, 1999), 71.

3. Horton, *We Believe*, 21.

4. Ryrie, *Basic Theology*, 26.

5. C. S. Lewis, *Mere Christianity* (New York: Macmillan, 1960), 56.

6. Charles Spurgeon, *Metropolitan Tabernacle Pulpit* (vol. 26, John 6:37), 118.

7. Norman Geisler, *Systematic Theology, Vol. 4* (Minneapolis: Bethany House, 2005), 94.

CULTURE

CHAPTER 14

Pastors Engaging the Culture

Defining the legalities of pastors and church leaders
to address political and social issues without fear of reprisal

by J. M. Smith

"Let each citizen remember at the moment he is offering his vote . . . that he is executing one of the most solemn trusts in human society for which he is accountable to God and his Country."
—Samuel Adams (April 16, 1781), father of the American Revolution and signer of the Declaration of Independence

The playing field has dramatically changed in America during the nearly two hundred thirty years since Sam Adams made his historic notation on the importance of voting and its relationship with Christian responsibility. We find ourselves in an environment wherein the mere mention of God and country can raise the hackles on modern "diversity" proponents who have no use for the absolutes of Christianity. In fact, if pastors in our nation were to follow the rules of church behavior as designed by the American Civil Liberties Union, Americans United for Separation of Church and State, the American Atheists, and other groups seeking to meticulously stifle religious expression, they would no doubt bury their heads in the proverbial sand and allow the culture to become a Christianity-free zone.

The fact is, however, that pastors are not required to shy away from political matters. Moreover, the rights of pastors to address cultural and political issues from their pulpit, and in other venues, are expressly protected. These chapters of *InnovateChurch* are designed to demonstrate to pastors and church leaders how to properly tackle political issues and to encourage them to be purveyors of "salt and light" ministries that jointly take aim at conducting evangelistic efforts and influencing the culture.

Let's kick off this chapter with five key questions.

Question 1: Is it legal for American churches to hold voter registration drives on their premises?

Answer: Absolutely. In fact, thousands of churches have legally held voter registration drives to ensure that their constituents are informed and ready to step into the voting booth. Such efforts began in the late 1970s with the foundation of the Moral Majority by Virginia pastor Jerry Falwell who understood the need for churches to address the nation's cultural nose-dive. That organization, which we'll highlight later in this chapter, was largely responsible for the election of President Ronald Reagan in 1980 and 1984 because of its concentrated voter registration efforts in churches.

Question 2: Is it legal for churches to distribute voting guides?

Answer: Again, absolutely. Churches may legally dispense nonpartisan voting guides that address candidates' records and issues.

Question 3: Is it legal for pastors to address political issues from the pulpit?

Answer: You guessed it. Absolutely. Pastors must be aware that churches simply may not devote more than a "substantial part" of their overall activity to addressing political issues, or lobbying.

Question 4: Is it legal for a pastor to endorse a political candidate?

Answer: As surprising as it may be, the answer is yes. Churches, on the other hand, may not offer endorsements of candidates. Similarly, pastors may make financial contributions to political candidates, as well as Political Action Committees (PACs), while churches may not.

Question 5: How many churches have lost their Internal Revenue Service (IRS) tax exemptions because they were deemed to have violated the IRS election regulations?

Answer: None. That's right, since 1954, when the political intervention restriction was added to the Internal Revenue Code (IRC), not one church has ever lost its tax-exempt status for engaging in political activity.

The significance of these answers is clear: there is no austere system of governmental regulations designed to limit the political speech of pastors and church leaders, even though the purveyors of abject secularism want us to believe that there is.

Political Snake Oil

Prior to the 2008 Iowa caucuses, some pastors who supported the presidential candidacy of former Arkansas Governor Mike Huckabee received a series of letters ominously warning them that their tax-exempt status would be threatened if they got involved in the caucus. One of the letters menacingly warned that Hawkeye State pastors could actually be jailed for supporting Mr. Huckabee's campaign. Another letter stated that the IRS was on the prowl for pastors who were violating federal tax rules regarding churches and elections. The Associated Press reported that one state pastor actually received nine letters warning him not to get involved in the campaign. The letters conveniently lacked any return addresses.

This was not the first time this type of intimidation tactic has been utilized. Americans United for Separation of Church and

State, which targets public religious expressions, has sent out, under its "Project Fair Play," letters attempting to stifle pastors. Again, this threat is made despite the fact that not one church in our nation's history has lost its tax-exempt status because of political activity. Nevertheless, the result of these types of disinformation campaigns may be that pastors become hesitant to address a political issue or social concern from the pulpit out of fear of retribution from a powerful civil liberties organization. Such fears are unnecessary. While the fact is that there are indeed groups that seek to silence pastors—often through dubious methods such as shadowy warning letters—pastors have a clear calling, as well as immutable rights to speak to the political and social issues of the day.

Toothless Scare Tactics

I recently sat down with Mathew Staver, the founder and chairman of Liberty Counsel who also serves as dean of Liberty University School of Law in Lynchburg, Virginia, to discuss with him the proper means by which pastors and churches may participate in the American political process. (Mat's wife, Anita, is president of Liberty Counsel, a nonprofit litigation, education, and policy organization dedicated to advancing religious freedom, the sanctity of human life, and the traditional family. Established in 1989, Liberty Counsel is a nationwide organization that has offices in Florida, Virginia, and Washington, D.C., and retains hundreds of affiliate attorneys across the nation.) Staver has a unique perspective on modern cultural/church issues because he at one time served as a pastor. Today he is a high-profile religious freedom warrior who has argued in numerous state and federal courts across the country, including the United States Supreme Court.

Staver says that threatening letters such as the ones sent to Iowa pastors are completely without merit. They are, he points out, merely scare tactics designed to silence Christian viewpoints. Pastors need to be aware that such letters have no meaning whatsoever and should be ignored.

"Do not be confused or intimated by such claims as found in these letters," Staver advises pastors and Christian leaders. He furthers this assertion by reminding pastors of their calling to confront the culture.

"Pastors and Christian ministry leaders," he says, "have a high calling to preach the truth from the Word of God. Speaking the truth is essential all the time, but it is especially important to do so when we elect leaders who will make law and policy that affect our faith, our families, and our freedom. There is an ongoing struggle for the soul of America. Many people look to pastors and Christian ministry leaders for guidance on important moral and social issues. Conversely, some people and organizations want pastors and Christian ministry leaders to remain silent while Rome burns."

In a nutshell, we see in this statement the environment in which pastors and church leaders often find themselves today. It is an increasingly hostile atmosphere wherein churches are expressly unwelcome. To understand how we arrived at this political crossroads, one must look back in history to the tenure of Thomas Jefferson, the third man to lead our nation as President. His words "a wall of separation," which at the time bore almost inconsequential meaning, have become an inflexible motto of the left. The axiom has been manipulated to the point that many believe it is a constitutional edict designed to prevent churches from having even a rudimentary influence in politics. Nothing could be further from the truth. The fact is that the phrase is found nowhere in the constitution and was originally written in a letter from Mr. Jefferson to a Baptist group in Danbury, Connecticut.

Basis of the Religious Freedom Wars

Written on New Year's Day, 1801, President Jefferson's letter read, in part: "Believing with you that religion is a matter which lies solely between Man & his God, that he owes account to none other for his faith or his worship, that the legitimate powers of government reach actions only, & not opinions, I contemplate with sovereign reverence that act of the whole American people which declared that *their* legislature should 'make no law respecting an establishment of religion, or prohibiting the free exercise thereof,' thus building a wall of separation between Church & State."[1]

Dr. Daniel L. Dreisbach, professor in the department of justice, law, and society at American University in Washington, D.C., believes Jefferson's letter has been narrow-mindedly sculpted to befit the abject desires of those who portray its message as one that promotes unyielding church-state separation. In his book *Thomas Jefferson and the Wall of Separation between Church and State,* Dr. Dreisbach argues that the purpose of Jefferson's "wall" metaphor was actually aimed at establishing separation not between church and civil government, but between federal and state governments. Jefferson certainly had views on religion that differed from his Federalist forerunners, and he thusly rejected federal proclamations on Thanksgiving and prayer. However, as governor of Virginia, he had signed a state-sanctioned Thanksgiving and prayer proclamation. It is interesting to note also that on Jefferson's grave marker, he wished to remind future generations of three of his greatest accomplishments. The marker reads: "Here was buried Thomas Jefferson, author of the Declaration of Independence, of the Statute of Virginia for Religious Freedom and father of the University of Virginia." Thomas Jefferson was not a stern enthusiast of ACLU-style religious repression and antagonism.

It should be noted too that the exploitation of the "wall" metaphor has not been universally accepted by jurists. Most notably, in one of the more dramatic challenges to its growing scope, a blunt dissent in 1985's *Wallace v. Jaffree* saw Justice William J. Rehnquist note that the modern interpretation of the phrase is based on bad history, has been an ineffective guide to judging, and should be rejected.

LBJ's Impact

The political landscape, as it pertained to churches, experienced its first major problem in 1954 when churches and other nonprofit organizations were halted from expressly endorsing or opposing candidates for political office. The change occurred when Texas World War II hero Lyndon Baines Johnson ran for reelection to the U.S. Senate. After easily winning reelection by a three-to-one margin, the vindictive Johnson, who had been opposed by a nonprofit organization (not a church), proposed legislation to amend the Internal Revenue Code so that it prohibited nonprofit organizations, including churches, from endorsing or opposing political candidates.

The code was amended that same year without any debate regarding the impact of the bill. The Internal Revenue Code to this day expressly prohibits churches and other nonprofit organizations from directly endorsing or opposing political candidates. However, from 1954 to the present, only one church has ever lost its IRS tax-exempt letter ruling. But even that church did not lose its tax-exempt status, as we'll see later in this chapter.

A key problem with LBJ's revised code was that it bolstered the future efforts of organizations that would one day begin the all-out assault on public religious expression, including the rights of churches to participate in the political process. While Roger Baldwin founded the ACLU in 1920, it wasn't until after the U.S. Supreme Court's infamous *Roe v. Wade* and *Doe v. Bolton* rulings—in which the Court held that the "right to privacy" includes a woman's right to have an abortion—that the ACLU and religious conservatives began to face off in what would become known as the "culture wars."

A Sleeping Giant Awakens

In the late 1970s, pastors Jerry Falwell, Tim LaHaye, D. James Kennedy, and Charles Stanley met with conservative political guru Paul Weyrich to discuss the possibility of launching a national religious-based organization that would contest upstart political and social issues that were facing the nation: abortion on demand, the breakdown of the family through divorce, the post-Summer of Love sexual promiscuity, and the collapse of our national security. The Moral Majority was born as a result of this meeting and it became an astounding political force that was largely responsible for the election of Ronald Reagan as president in 1980.

While the organization was typically cast as a gathering of backwoods Bible thumpers, the organization welcomed a wide base of support and literally redefined the cultural landscape. Pastors and conservative Americans, primarily churchgoers, had arisen from the dust of political inactivity to become a powerful voting bloc. And with the dramatic success of the Moral Majority came reflex opposition. That resistance continues to this day, often in the form of disinformation campaigns aimed at churches, like those seen in Iowa.

The Giant Sleeps Again

And so we return to the present day where the ACLU and similar groups have instigated an aggressive campaign designed to stifle public religious expression. This campaign is based almost entirely on the murky "wall of separation" metaphor that has come to define the movement that seeks to restrain public religious expression while ignoring, even deceptively redefining, our nation's obvious Judeo-Christian heritage.

Why are Christians the focus of such stern opposition that includes the highlighted disinformation campaigns? The answer lies in the sheer volume of our numbers. There are today an estimated fifty-two million evangelical Christians in America who are eligible to vote. And while only thirty-three million (or sixty percent) of evangelicals actually voted in the 2004 general election and only about twenty million (or thirty-nine percent) voted in 2006, the potential for a Reaganesque turnout at the polls is always possible, especially if an opposing presidential candidate jolts this voting bloc into panicked action.

As Mat Staver noted in our conversations, "If the culture war is to be won and America to be restored 'under God,' Christians must register and vote in far greater numbers."

The Church at Pierce Creek

And so we see the need for churches to remain politically active. As noted at the beginning of this chapter, churches have great leeway in terms of participating in the political process. Here is a great example of pastors working together to affect the culture. The Ohio Restoration Project's "Patriot Pastors" project, which includes about one thousand state pastors, seeks to register voters and prepare fellow Christians to become "salt and light for America." The Restoration Project this year distributed about five hundred thousand copies of its voter guide, identifying candidates' positions on key issues such as abortion. All of this is perfectly legal.

But let's examine now what pastors may *not* do, in terms of political activity. To understand what should not be done, we need look no further than the 1992 actions of the Binghamton, N.Y.-based Church at Pierce Creek. During that year's presidential campaign, the church placed full-page ads in *USA TODAY* and the *Washington Times* to announce its opposition to then-Arkansas Governor Bill Clinton's campaign.

The Church at Pierce Creek became the first (and only!) church to ever lose its IRS letter ruling. Because the ads were sponsored by the church and donations were solicited, the IRS revoked the church's letter ruling, but *not* its tax-exempt status.

The Church at Pierce Creek then sued, arguing that the IRS had violated its free-speech rights. Ultimately an appellate court upheld a federal court ruling that found that churches are tax exempt without an IRS letter ruling. The court noted that "because of the unique treatment churches receive under the Internal Revenue Code, the impact of the revocation is likely to be more symbolic than substantial." So not even the Church at Pierce Creek lost its tax-exempt status, and not one donor was affected by this incident.

We see in this example that churches may not endorse or oppose candidates for elective office. Again, this is the primary focus that churches should avoid. As noted earlier, pastors may address political issues in a variety of ways: preaching on biblical and moral issues, such as traditional marriage and abortion; urging their congregations to register and vote; reviewing the positions of candidates, within a church setting; and personally endorsing candidates. Further, churches are afforded the right to engage in many political activities, including: distributing nonpartisan voter guides; registering voters; providing transportation to the polls; holding candidate forums; and introducing visiting candidates.

As far as voter guides go, during election seasons several organizations publish valuable voter guides, including Faith2Action (www.f2a.org); WallBuilders (www.wallbuilders.com); and the Christian Coalition of America (www.cc.org/voterguides.cfm). Other recommended sites include Liberty Counsel (www.lc.org), the Campaign for Working Families (www.campaignforfamilies.org), the American Family Association's Legislative Action Center (http://capwiz.com/afanet/dbq/officials), the Family Research Council (www.frc.org) and Concerned Women for America (www.cwfa.org).

Churches and the IRS

Now let's quickly examine the difference between an IRS tax-exempt letter ruling and tax-exempt status of churches. Staver says that every organization, whether a 501(c)(4) (a nonprofit group that primarily lobbies) or a 501(c)(3) (a nonprofit, tax-exempt organization), must file an application with the IRS to be recognized as a nonprofit organization for purposes of the Internal Revenue Code. The IRS then issues a letter ruling specific for the organization, in which the federal agency acknowledges that the organization will be recognized as a nonprofit organization, and in the case of a 501(c)(3), that contributions to the organization will be tax-deductible.

Staver adds that, unlike virtually every other nonprofit or tax-exempt organization, churches are not required to obtain an IRS letter ruling. Some churches have an IRS letter and some do not. He says that there is no advantage of a church having a letter ruling, as opposed to a church that does not have one. The only difference, he says, is one of convenience. For example, if a donor is ever audited and the IRS questioned the contributions to the church, the donor could point the agent to the letter ruling on file with the IRS. However, Staver says that if a church doesn't have a letter ruling, it can merely produce an affidavit by the pastor, or present the church's bylaws or other evidence to validate that the assembly is indeed a church.

Pastors and church leaders may wish to visit the section of the IRS Web site that highlights tax information for charitable organizations (www.irs.gov/charities/charitable/index.html).

Representatives of Christ

Elias Boudinot (1800–1839), the renowned newspaperman who was translating the Bible into Cherokee when he was killed, said, "Good government generally begins in the family, and if the moral character of a people once degenerate, their political character must soon follow."[2]

That statement remains pertinent today, and it behooves Christians to be persistently carrying out the words of 2 Chronicles 7:14: "[If] My people who are called by My name humble themselves, pray and seek My face, and turn from their evil ways, then I will hear from heaven, forgive their sin, and heal their land." This verse suggests that Christians should be actively working to elect national leaders who will seek to protect our national Judeo-Christian values.

Mathew Staver tirelessly works to urge pastors to be determined representatives of Christ, even within the political realm. "Pastors should throw away the muzzles that some wish to impose on them and replace them with megaphones," he says. "It was sermons of pastors that fueled the American Revolution. America needs her pastors to once again speak up and address the religious and moral issues of the day. It is far more likely to be struck by lightning twice than for churches to lose their tax-exempt status over political issues."[3]

To help pastors fulfill their high calling of fearlessly speaking the truth of the gospel, Liberty Counsel provides free information addressing what pastors and churches may legally do with respect to political candidates and lobbying. Pastors or church leaders having additional questions or a need for advice may call 800-671-1776 or visit www.LC.org for more information on these and other religious freedom issues. Liberty Counsel also provides a complimentary DVD titled, "Pastors, Churches, and Political Activity," that is available upon request.

Notes

1. See Breisback book.
2. Source unknown.
3. Interview between J. M. Smith and Mathew Staver.

CHAPTER 15

The Ins and Outs of Engaging the Culture

by Mat Staver

On March 4, 2008, I presented oral argument at the California Supreme Court in San Francisco, speaking in favor of upholding the state marriage law. The scene that day was surreal. Through Liberty Counsel, I have been involved in front-line ministry to preserve marriage as the union of one man and one woman. Who would have thought a decade ago that the definition of marriage would come under attack? The problem lies at the feet of activist judges who base their opinions on personal whims.

Churches and the Culture

A primary reason we are seeing an ongoing collapse of our national morals is because pastors, church leaders, and congregations are often unwilling to get their hands dirty in order to represent biblical values in tough cultural challenges.

Those are hard-hitting words, I know. But the fact is that churches and other nonprofit, tax-exempt organizations may actively promote the passage of state and federal marriage amendments. There is no reason to steer clear of marriage initiatives or other cultural issues.

New Challenges for the Faithful

The need for Liberty Counsel is evident. Every year we take on cases wherein we represent people whose religious freedoms have been curtailed. From our inception until 2004, Liberty Counsel was blessed with an 86 percent win ratio. Since 2004 we have won 92 percent of our cases. These are typically not routine cases, and many times our victories have a direct impact on the culture and the future of America.

In the recent past, to name just a few of our cases, we have represented:

- kids in Good News school-based clubs who have been hit with discriminatory usage fees
- a student who was told he could not include an image of Jesus on a school art project
- churches that have faced discriminatory zoning ordinances
- a school choir that was barred from performing Christmas songs
- a Christian businessman facing a lawsuit because he refused to reproduce a homosexual-themed video that countered his beliefs
- churches fighting the ACLU, which sought to have certain property tax exemptions revoked
- students who were told they could not pass out material bearing Scripture at school
- new Christian inmates wishing to be baptized

- participants at a community center who were told that religious meetings were unconstitutional
- students who were suspended for peacefully praying before school
- backers of "Choose Life" license plates that promote adoption over abortion
- proponents of "informed consent" laws that require information about their unborn child to be given to women considering abortion before undergoing the procedure

Silence Is Not an Option

In one of our celebrated cases, Liberty Counsel represented Megan Chapman, a Russell Springs, Kentucky, senior who was told by a federal court that she could not pray at her graduation.

But on the day of that graduation, something amazing occurred. Prior to Megan's speech, the entire senior class rose as one body and recited "The Lord's Prayer" in a wonderfully emotional scene. Megan, who was planning only to read the poem, "The Road Less Traveled," put away her notes as she approached the podium. And she began to speak from her heart. Megan talked about her faith in Jesus Christ and talked of how He regularly strengthens and encourages her. Incredibly the crowd gave her several standing ovations. The local media described the event as having a "revival-like atmosphere."

Later Megan was able to give her testimony on the FOX News Channel and in other media venues. This challenge to her faith allowed her to speak about Jesus in ways she never dreamed possible. In this instance, we see that a young girl who was willing to be a representative of Christ, even when she faced great opposition, learned that God shows Himself to be true. He will open amazing doors of opportunity when we are bold representatives of His gospel.

Megan is today a student at Liberty University and is preparing to become an attorney who will represent kids like her who face discrimination solely because of their desire to publicly represent their faith in Jesus Christ.

(Let me add this as an aside: student speech delivered on religious themes during graduation, when the content is not compelled by school officials, is protected by the First Amendment. When students elect a classmate to give a message of his/her choice, it is unconstitutional to censor a religious viewpoint. While the senior class eventually engaged in spontaneous prayer and Megan's speech contained religious themes, the court should never have issued an order instructing her not to pray.)

Willing Vessels

I believe God is looking for many willing vessels like Megan Chapman who will selflessly and courageously be "salt and light" ambassadors of the faith within the culture. Our culture cries out for representatives of the gospel who will stand up against the advancing tide of secularism that seeks to stifle all public religious expression, especially expression of the Judeo-Christian origin. We need an informed and motivated church populace that is willing to take a stand for the values that have defined this nation since its inception.

That's where Liberty Counsel comes in. In addition to our extensive legal work, we frequently make available a large variety of educational materials to pastors, students, teachers, nonprofit organizations, and others who need legal assistance. We also send out a "Liberty Alert" e-mail to inform subscribers about breaking news of current cases impacting religious freedom, the sanctity of human life, and the traditional family.

Further, the Liberty Center for Law & Policy (LCLP) operates as another component of Liberty Counsel's training, education, and public policy program. With offices in Washington, D.C., and on the campus of the Liberty University School of Law in Lynchburg,

Virginia, the LCLP trains attorneys, law students, policy makers, legislators, clergy, and world leaders in constitutional principles and government policies.

As you can see, we are involved in exciting new programs that are designed to advance religious liberty, the sanctity of human life, and the traditional family. And if you think the church doesn't need to impact our society, let me point out a few more cases in which we have been involved:

- We won a case on appeal where a trial judge ruled that sex and gender are in the mind, granting child custody to a transsexual.
- We settled a lawsuit against a school district and stopped the first homosexual high school in America.
- We won a series of huge marriage victories in New York, California, Tennessee, Connecticut, and Nebraska, and defended marriage as the union of one man and one woman in more than forty separate legal cases.

These cases have a direct bearing on the church. You see, if our society accepts the notion that sex and gender are "only in the mind," how can pastors hope to bring biblical messages on God's design for traditional marriage? We can see that the long-term effect of these types of cases could have a harmful effect on the church.

Christian Community at Work

Liberty Counsel cooperates and coordinates its efforts with other religious liberty, pro-life, and pro-family organizations. We have represented many notable clients, including: Focus on the Family; Child Evangelism Fellowship; Dr. Jerry Falwell and Liberty University; and the Christian Educators Association International.

We believe that like-minded groups should cooperate, but that we should not all become one group. (Eccles. 4:9, 12: "Two are better than one . . . [and] a cord of three stands is not easily broken.")

We love to work with churches and Christian organizations in affecting our culture. For example, we have worked with:

- Exodus International in offering practical and biblical insights on how both individuals and churches can become a haven for those who are seeking freedom from same-sex attraction;
- Child Evangelism Fellowship in protecting the Bible-based programs of Good News clubs across the country;
- the Institute for Creation Research in equipping believers with evidence of the Bible's accuracy and authority through scientific research and educational programs conducted within a biblical framework,
- and many more.

We must be willing to fearlessly and compassionately confront cultural issues from a biblical perspective.

I see this as a biblical imperative. I don't think we can claim the promises of 2 Chronicles 7:14 unless we are involved in active ministry to the culture.

Cultural Crossroads

In recent times I believe the situation at the College of William & Mary in Williamsburg, Virginia, is a picture of the hopelessness being offered by some to members of our society. At the school, President Gene R. Nichol showed vast intolerance toward Christianity while at the same time sanctioning a shocking sex program at the school.

Mr. Nichol removed a historic cross in the school's Wren Chapel because of concerns that the symbol might be offensive to some students. The cross of Christ was removed because it was seen as a potentially offensive emblem. In a separate but related matter, Mr. Nichol also approved a "Sex Workers' Art Show," which featured porn stars and strippers, on the W&M campus.

I see this dichotomy as a picture of an American society that, while increasingly hostile to our Judeo-Christian traditions, simultaneously promotes sexual experimentation and sexual ambiguity. As our nation turns its back on the foundational truths of the Bible, it is also belligerently accepting and consenting to social policies that are anathema to the very values being shunned. It is a vicious and endless cycle that can only result in national tragedy.

In the W&M case, Mr. Nichol resigned after receiving notice that his contract would not be renewed by the college's Board of Visitors. Following the removal of the cross and the authorization of the controversial sex show, the college reported losing a $12 million gift. That sealed Mr. Nichol's fate.

Prior to Mr. Nichol's resignation, Liberty Counsel sent a letter to W&M Chancellor and former U.S. Supreme Court Justice Sandra Day O'Connor, stating that the removal of the cross from the chapel was unnecessary and unconstitutional. (Mr. Nichol later announced a weak compromise, saying the cross would be returned on Sundays, during Christian religious services, or when requested by a visitor.)

It is apparent that on many of our nation's college campuses, open hostility toward religion is a way of life. Thankfully many young Christian students are actively living out their faith on their campuses, despite frequent opposition. These students refuse to be pressured into abandoning their faith in Christ. Their energy is what we need in our congregations because I believe the effort to silence Christians will one day result in a direct assault on churches.

"Faith-Based" Dilemma

Many Christian ministries are already in the crosshairs of groups like the ACLU. Take for example the Iowa InnerChange Freedom Initiative (IFI), which is a faith-based pre-release program for prisoners with exemplary records of successfully rehabilitating hardened criminals into successful members of society. The problem is that little term "faith-based."

On June 2, 2006, after a lawsuit was brought by the Americans United for the Separation of Church and State, a judge ordered the program to be shut down and that IFI and its affiliate, Prison Fellowship Ministries, repay the state $1.5 million that it had received for services over a six-year period. In his ruling, the judge labeled IFI "pervasively sectarian," which he said made the $1.5 million in funds a violation of the separation of church and state. An appeals process is in the works.

The celebrated success of this Christian ministry apparently did not matter to this judge. All that seemingly matters is that a secular group believed that a faith-based organization should not be receiving state funds to help in the rehabilitation of prisoners. It is apparent that there is a culture war in our nation and Christians and Christian ministries are being targeted.

America Needs Activists

America is a gift from God. Therefore, how can God's people not fight to protect the wonderful freedom that this nation affords us?

Noah Webster stated,

> When you become entitled to exercise the right of voting [remember] that God commands you to choose for rulers "just men who will rule in fear of God." The preservation of [our] government depends on the faithful discharge of this Duty and place unprincipled men in office, the government will soon be corrupted; laws will be made, not for the public good so much as for selfish or local purposes; corrupt or incompetent men will be appointed to execute the Laws; the public revenues will be squandered on unworthy men; and the rights of the citizen will be violated or disregarded. If [our] government fails to

secure public prosperity and happiness, it must be
because the citizens neglect the Divine Commands,
and elect bad men to make and administer the
Laws.[1]

Those words are a picture of today, as many bad laws are
being respectively made and interpreted by disingenuous law-
makers and jurists who have forsaken biblical values in favor of
ever-shifting social impulses. America's pastors and churches must
be in the business of calling this nation back to God.

While this book is about church innovations, I actually don't
see a need for a great deal of innovation in terms of church activism. That's because, in this regard, real innovation took place
more than a quarter-century ago. I see a need for a resurgence
of the old-fashioned passion of cultural heroes who entered the
fires of activism in the 1970s and 1980s. People such as: Moral
Majority founder Jerry Falwell; theologian and cultural activist
Dr. Francis Schaeffer; Christian statesman Dr. D. James Kennedy;
Concerned Women for America founder Dr. Beverly LaHaye;
Dr. Tim LaHaye; and many others. They were the innovators. And
we must look to their example now as we accept the challenge to
again confront the culture of our own day.

I encourage pastors and church leaders and people in the pews
of our nation's churches to determine that we must take a stand for
the cause of Christ in our nation. While we are working to reach
souls with the gospel of Christ, we must also be engaged in battle
to preserve our religious freedom.

At the beginning of this chapter, I observed that ten years ago
few people could have imagined that we would be involved in a
host of legal battles against same-sex marriage. Can you imagine
what our culture may be facing in another ten years? Will same-sex
marriage be a way of life in our nation? Will the same-sex marriage
culture be pervasive in our schools? Will churches be compelled
to perform same-sex ceremonies because local or state ordinances
prohibit "discrimination"?

Other cultural questions persist: Will the rights of parents continue to be whittled away, specifically in terms of "abortion rights" for their minor daughters? Will the anti-Christian climate in many of our public schools accelerate to the point where students of faith are completely silenced and ostracized? Will our public squares become sanitized to the point that Ten Commandments monuments and other Judeo-Christian symbols are fully outlawed?

I don't believe that these are farfetched questions. And while I cannot predict the future, I do know that we need take only a cursory look at the ongoing cultural decline in our nation to see that America is becoming less welcoming toward Christianity. This is not a time for timidity. It is readily apparent that the culture wars are in full swing, and it is imperative that we raise up a new generation of Christians who are willing to step into the battle.

Notes

1. Need source for Noah Webster quote.

PRAYER

CHAPTER 16

Innovative Prayer in the Local Church

by Daniel Henderson

The Russian scientist Ivan Pavlov was awarded the Nobel Prize in Physiology (Medicine) in 1904 for his studies of the digestive system. He is most famous for his experiments with dogs whose saliva glands could be activated by conditioning. He found that the dogs associated food with the lab coats of the scientists who fed them. Over time, dogs would salivate at the sight of the lab coat, even if there was no food in proximity. The same was true of the ringing of a bell, used consistently in association with feeding time. Ring the bell and the dogs would drool.

Pavlov's discovery was that environmental events that previously had no relation to a given reflex (such as a bell sound) could, through experience, trigger a reflex (salivation). This kind of learned response is called conditioned reflex.

Many Christians have a conditioned reflex to the idea of prayer. That reflex is to yawn. This is not because prayer is inherently boring. It is because our failure to pray effectively, earnestly, and energetically has conditioned many church members to respond to the call with recollections of stodgy prayer times marked by drudgery and fatigue.

As I have the occasion to travel across the nation calling churches into fresh experiences of innovative prayer, I find an astounding amount of entrenched boredom. In many circles, the mere mention of a prayer time almost assures a low attendance.

Most of us would not admit it, but at one point or another we've concluded that prayer can be a very sleepy experience. Yet, communion with the Creator should never be boring and the incredible privilege of prayer never neglected.

Our Struggle for Quantity in Prayer

Our need for a fresh infusion of biblical, balanced, and innovative prayer in the American church is significant. Without this kind of movement, we will never reach the full potential of His power in our lives or experience the revival we desperately need in our churches.

Jon Graf, founding editor of *Pray!* magazine and director of the National Association of Local Church Prayer Leaders, estimates that only five percent of all American churches have a significant, mobilized prayer ministry.[1] Of course every church prays, but not all churches are noted as a "praying church." Many have prayer activities but not a prayer culture that permeates all they do.

In a survey of almost a thousand pastors, pollster George Barna discovered the minimal place of prayer in the current philosophy of ministry among many churches. When asked about the most important ministry emphases in their church at the dawn of a new calendar year, pastors listed prayer very last as vital to their plans for health and growth.[2]

Clearly the quantity of prayer in the American church falls far short of Jesus' vision that His house be distinguished as a house of prayer (see Mark 11:17). When Paul gave Timothy divinely inspired instructions about the priorities and structure of the local church, he boldly proclaimed, "First of all, then, I urge that . . . prayers . . . be made for everyone" (1 Tim. 2:1).

Our Struggle with Quality in Prayer

Perhaps one reason we struggle with quantity is that the quality of our praying can be quite pitiful. Many of the prayer meetings I attended as a child and even participate in occasionally today are . . . well, boring!

I distinctly remember the good old-fashioned prayer times of my youth. Some were not "prayer meetings" at all. They were Bible studies with minimal prayer tacked on the end of the gathering.

When we did pray, we seemed to get stuck in a rut of requests. After a few perfunctory songs, we asked the dreaded question: "Does anyone have any prayer requests?" And it went on, and on, and on. After forty-five minutes of horizontal discussion, I thought everyone in the country had an ingrown toenail, a friend with a slipped disc, a cousin with cancer, or a neighbor in financial crisis. I was so depressed I did not feel like praying.

Sometimes these gatherings became more like gossip sessions than prayer times. Often, much of the "sharing" was checkered with details about the juicy tidbits of everyone's marriage, health, or family problems. At the end we prayed rapidly over all the scribbles on the yellow pads, pronouncing a hurried "bless" or "be with" over each item. When it was all said and done (more "said" than "done"), I concluded that if that was God's idea of a dynamic, biblical prayer time, then something was really amuck with the whole idea. I felt like crying out, "We've fallen and we can't get up!"

God Is Not the Author of Boredom

After twenty-five years of pastoral ministry, leading multiple prayer meetings every week, I have concluded that God is not the author of boredom, especially when we are conversing with

Him. Over the decades I have been in prayer meetings (and even led some) where participants drooled, fell over, snored, and even snorted. In my book *PRAYzing! An A to Z Guide to Creative Prayer,* I declare war on sleepy prayer times. If prayer lacks creativity, energy, and innovation, it is not God's fault; it is ours.[3]

Admittedly, we've all engaged in many "supplication siestas." Even Peter, James, and John dozed off in the garden (see Matt. 26:36–42). Like them, our spirit is willing, but our flesh is weak.

Yet, the New Testament commands us to be watchful, wakeful, and alert in prayer (see Eph. 6:18; Col. 4:2; 1 Pet. 4:7). How do we find the keys to energized, engaging prayer? As a pastor, my frustration with lethargic, dozy gatherings has motivated me to try and learn more about how to avoid these dead-in-the-water prayer times. Over the years I have learned a lot about creative approaches to prayer. There is still much to learn, but this chapter will help us all to avoid nodding off in the prayer room.

The Possibilities of Innovative Prayer

The Bible gives us a foundation for a fresh expectation, exploration, energy, and experience in prayer. To discover these elements, we turn to the first few chapters of the word of God.

The Expectation of Innovation (Praying to a Creative God)

A. W. Tozer's famous quote is profoundly relevant as we consider the beginning place of effective prayer. He noted, "The most important thing about a person is what comes to mind when they think about God." So, what comes to mind when we think about praying to God? Is He a temperamental old man with a big club He wields when we mess up? Is He a jolly, terrestrial Santa Claus dumping any and all goodies in those who behave? Certainly He is Father, a fortress, good and loving toward His children.

We all know the English Bible begins with these words: "In the beginning God created." This first action in all of human history is also the original description of His character. I suggest we make this a foundational presumption every time we pray. God's name in Genesis 1:1 is *Elohim*. "Creative glory and power and God-head fullness are associated with this initial name in the Bible . . . in *Elohim*, God is the majestic Ruler, and under such a name we have the idea of omnipotence, or creative and governing power."[4]

The closer you look and the broader you travel, the more you begin to fill up your cup of understanding from the ocean of His creativity. In my travels I've been awed by the grandeur of the Rockies, the crystal blue waters of Hawaii, the varied fruits and flowers of Indonesia, the fantastic wildlife of Africa, and spectacular brilliance of the Northern Lights.

Our expectations for prayer are ignited when we realize we pray to the One who created it all. As Psalm 96:5–6 declares, "But the LORD made the heavens. Splendor and majesty are before Him; strength and beauty are in His sanctuary." As we pray to a creative God, we can expect and experience splendor, majesty, strength, and beauty.

The Exploration for Innovation (Praying from the Creative Word)

Psalm 33:6 tells us, "The heavens were made by the word of the LORD, and all the stars, by the breath of His mouth." In the creation account, God spoke and creative power was unleashed. Today He still speaks to us through Christ the living word (Heb. 1:1–3) and His powerful written word (see Heb. 4:12).

I do not always have a Bible opened every time I pray, but in the normal course of my daily time with the Lord I always start with an open Bible. Several times a week I lead collective prayer gatherings. Every prayer time starts with the Scriptures. When I facilitate three-day prayer summits (which I will describe later), Scripture is the primary prayer tool giving fresh insight, inspiration, and articulation to our prayers. We never run out of prayer material.

By conviction and experience I have concluded that the most creative and effective prayers spring from the inexhaustible treasury of the Word of God. Thousands of times I have watched the Bible expose hearts, guide language, unite diverse interests, and create indescribably powerful moments of remarkable prayer impact.

Eugene Peterson said it well: "We restore prayer to its context in God's word. Prayer is not something we think up to get God's attention or enlist His favor. Prayer is answering speech. The first word is God's word. Prayer is a human word and is never the first word, never the primary word, never the initiating and shaping word simply because we are never first; never primary . . . the first word everywhere and always is God's word to us, not ours to Him."[5]

The best way to talk to God is in His own words. They are inspired, creative, and powerful words that provide a limitless exploration for innovative prayer.

The Energy for Innovation (Praying by the Creative Spirit)

Genesis 1:2 tells us the triune God looked over a formless, dark, and empty mass. The Spirit of God "hovered" over the amorphous abyss of raging, chaotic waters. I love the word picture of the Spirit "hovering" or "brooding" over the waters. The Hebrew word means "to move gently, to softly brood" or even "to fertilize."

Suddenly, at the will and voice of God, light appeared. Soon, all that we know existed in fullness, order, and beauty. When we pray we must remember that, if we are born-again, that Spirit lives in our hearts. The truth of God's word is the fuel for the Spirit's innovative invitations to prayer.

As we are led by the Spirit in our prayer times (see Rom. 8:14) we can step outside the box of all the lazy, dozy, cozy prayer times we have experienced in the past. God's Word makes this promise:

> but just as it is written, "THINGS WHICH EYE HAS NOT SEEN AND EAR HAS NOT HEARD, AND which

HAVE NOT ENTERED THE HEART OF MAN, ALL THAT
GOD HAS PREPARED FOR THOSE WHO LOVE HIM." For
to us God revealed them through the Spirit; for the
Spirit searches all things, even the depths of God.
For who among men knows the thoughts of a man
except the spirit of the man which is in him? Even
so the thoughts of God no one knows except the
Spirit of God. Now we have received, not the spirit
of the world, but the Spirit who is from God, so that
we may know the things freely given to us by God.
(1 Cor. 2:9–12 NASB).

This is our confidence and energy for long-term innovative,
engaging prayer. The Spirit is our indwelling tutor in prayer
(see Rom. 8:26–27) and will reveal to us the depth, sufficiency,
and application of His Word. When is this more necessary than in
our prayer times?

Over the years I've had the privilege of overseeing more
than 40 local church prayer summits. These three-day prayer
events involve Christians coming away from the business of life
to a retreat center. We've had groups from 15 to 225. There is no
agenda, only a variety of prayer expressions fueled by spontaneous
Scripture reading, a cappella singing, responsive prayer, and intercession. They are truly the most life-changing prayer experiences
I have ever witnessed.

Yet, time after time, I have felt and watched the Holy Spirit
take the powerful truths of the Word of God and lead us in innovated expressions of prayer that were energizing, convicting, par-
ticipatory, and transforming.

The Experience of Innovation (Praying in a Creative Way)

Looking again at Genesis, we discover God's design in creating mankind with these words, "Let Us make man in Our image,
according to Our likeness" (1:26). Among other possibilities, we

must conclude that this "image" entails a profound and abound-ing creativity. Observe that a few verses later, God allows Adam to name all the animals in the garden. Imagine the moment. He can make up any syllable, vowel, guttural sound, or combination thereof that he wishes. This is a picture of profound creativity unleashed as Adam walks and works in perfect communion with His Creator.

Today as we seek to enliven the prayer life and raise the prayer level of our churches, let us remember our origins. Let us consider our ancestor as he named the animals with unleashed imagina-tion, springing from his intimacy with his God. Like Adam, we are made in God's image. His written Word and indwelling Spirit now instruct us. The possibilities are vast as we commune with the Father.

So when we pray, we should be innovative, just like God. It's who He is in us. It is what He made us to do.

The Practices of Innovative Prayer

At Thomas Road Baptist Church and Liberty University, thousands are experiencing a fresh interest in prayer. Of course, the church has a powerful history of prayer dating back to the founding days in the 1950s, as Jerry Falwell sought the Lord dili-gently for direction and blessing. Many periods of extraordinary prayer and fasting have marked the advancement of the ministry. Seasoned intercessors are still very active in carrying the momen-tum of the church forward on their knees. Yet, new expressions of prayer are springing up as biblical teaching and hungry hearts continue to fuel a movement of seeking after God.

Worship-Based Approach: One of the most powerful prin-ciples that fuels innovative prayer is the teaching of worship-based prayer. As I have noted, I grew up in a tradition of "request-based" prayer.

Peter Lord, a well-known (now retired) Southern Baptist pastor, created "The 29:59 Prayer Guide," which sold more than

600,000 copies in the two decades after its release in 1976. Now it has been revised and is available in a fresh design.[6] This prayer plan teaches believers the idea of worship-based prayer. Pastor Lord recently told me, "Most Christians pray from a grocery list or out of crisis." In this, Pastor Lord is reflecting on a longing for us as Christians to learn to pray from a foundation of worship, not just requests.

While requests are a component of prayer, they are not the foundation. According to the model Jesus gave in Matthew 6:9–13 the starting place of prayer is worship ("Our Father in heaven, Your name be honored as holy. . . ."). This worship focus is followed by surrender to the will and kingdom purposes of God (v. 10). Then we are ready to trust the Lord with our requests for provision (v. 11) and relational purity (v. 12). We then trust the Lord for His victory as we face the temptations and trials of the daily journey (v. 13). This pattern is found in "The 29:59 Prayer Guide" and is being taught with greater popularity today.

Worship-based prayer focuses on God's face (who He is) while request-based prayer focuses on His hand (what He does for us). Both are good and important. However, I have learned that if we only focus on His hand, we may miss His face. Conversely, if we focus on His face, He is always glad to open His hand.

Prayer is enlivened and energized by worship-based prayer, especially when that worship springs from the Word of God. In many prayer meetings at Thomas Road Baptist Church, we begin with an open Bible, typically reading a psalm. The first question we ask is: "What does this passage tell us about God and His character?" Then we take the next several minutes and give God the praise, honor, and thanks that He is due, based on the Scripture passage. We do this through spoken reflections or songs. We do not ask for anything. Asking comes later.

This approach opens up profound insight, personal responses, and powerful expressions of need as we put the Lord, not the grocery list, first. We are learning that our creative God is honored,

His creative word is utilized, His creative Spirit is active, and our creative prayers abound.

Practical, Compelling Training: One essential aspect for fueling a movement of innovative prayer is ongoing biblical training. Recently TRBC hosted a two-day seminar designed to teach ministry leaders how to lead exciting, biblical prayer times. Almost 750 church and university leaders attended. Each is now better equipped to ignite fresh expressions of prayer in their respective circles of influxes.

Each Wednesday evening Dr. Elmer Towns teaches a faithful group of church members how to experience fresh insights in prayer. Adult Bible Fellowship classes are utilized to teach participants innovative ways of praying with one another in prayer partnerships, families, and ministry units. Parents are taught to pray for their children, and many other targeted types of intercession are featured in a variety of training experiences.

Prayer Summits: A newer expression of prayer is the multi-day prayer summits. Already the students at Liberty University have enjoyed this extraordinary form of innovative and protracted prayer. Most summits are occurring within the ministry, targeting men, women, and ministry leaders.

These three-day retreats feature Scripture-fed, Spirit-led prayer. There is no agenda, only some basic guidelines. Trained facilitators give general direction to the prayer times. Every participant is invited to read Scripture aloud, begin songs, and pray in the areas of focus suggested by the facilitators. The retreats feature large-group times, small gender-specific prayer huddles, prayer walking, codes of silence, and many other fresh expressions of prayer. Most participants attend a summit, wondering how they could ever pray for three days. Almost all leave wondering how the time flew by so quickly. This truly becomes a watermark of prayer experience and is teaching people how to pray in new ways and practice patterns that help them throughout their lives.

Interactive Prayer Stations: Another form of prayer, especially popular with the college students, involves interactive prayer stations. These stations are utilized regularly in communion services and all-night prayer meetings. Each station typically features a theme, based on Scripture, and a practical way to engage in a hands-on prayer exercise. Some might involve writing a prayer request, a praise, the name of an unsaved friend, or the decryption of a part of the world for which a student may have a burden. Some involve various uses of candles, water, sand, art supplies, journals, or even food. The sky is the limit but the enjoyment and participation are profound.

Glow Stick Prayer: Another movement of innovative prayer involves glow sticks. Every Sunday night students gather in the vicinity of the prayer chapel on campus to worship, pray, and raise their glow sticks as a symbol of their desire to be broken, then experience and express the glory of Christ in the world. The Glow Stick Prayer Service Facebook page reads: "We're begging God to break us, break our campus, break the surrounding areas and ultimately sweep across this nation. . . . We don't need to ask God to move. He is moving, and He has been moving this whole time. We need to move!"

Led by students, Glow Stick encourages corporate and private prayer along with times of worship or a brief message. Different themes are chosen for various Sunday nights, such as choosing one person to pray for throughout the week or praying for God to work in a specific way in one's life. Students can even be seen wearing actual glow sticks around campus, both as a reminder to pray and to further promote the prayer service.

Limitless Expressions: Many more innovative prayer experiences are springing up regularly. More ideas can be found in other writings by the staff and faculty.[7] We hope you will join us in the discovery that because we pray to a good and faithful Creator, who provides all we need to enjoy His presence, we never need to be bored again when we pray.

Notes

1. Daniel Henderson, *Fresh Encounters—Experiencing Transformation Through United Worship-based Prayer* (Colorado Springs: NavPress, 2003), 47.

2. *The Barna Update: Church Priorities for 2005 Vary Considerably* (Ventura: The Barna Report, February 14, 2005).

3. Daniel Henderson, *PRAYzing! Creative Prayer Experiences from A to Z* (Colorado Springs: NavPress; 2007), 21.

4. Herbert Lockyer, *All the Divine Names and Titles of the Bible* (Grand Rapids: Zondervan, 1988), 6.

5. Eugene Peterson, *Working the Angles* (Grand Rapids: Erdmann, 1987), 47.

6. *The 29:59 Prayer Guide Revisioned* (Forest, VA: Strategic Renewal), www.pray2959.com.

7. Elmer Towns and Daniel Henderson, *The Church That Prays Together—Inside the Prayer Life of 10 Dynamic Churches* by (Colorado Springs: NavPress, 2008).

CHAPTER 17

Innovate: Faith-Praying

Jerry Falwell's life of impassioned prayer and audacious faith

by Elmer Towns

D id you know that Jerry Falwell's boyhood home was located on the east end of the mountain that is today home of Liberty University? As a young boy, Jerry walked every path on that mountain while hunting for squirrels and rabbits. After Jerry had planted Thomas Road Baptist Church (1957) and God began to call him to start a Christian college, Jerry began walking across every part of that mountain, claiming it as the place for a great Christian training center that would reach the world.

Today Liberty University is the largest evangelical school in the world and is impacting the culture in amazing ways. That mountain is today known as Liberty Mountain. (And Jerry's boyhood home is still there. His twin brother Gene and his wife live in it.)

We see in this story the embodiment of bold faith and bold vision. Jerry faithfully walked that mountain before he had any money to pay for purchasing it and he claimed it by faith when the student body had only a few hundred students that were meeting in areas across Lynchburg. He didn't have enough students to utilize the mountain in those early days, but God had plans for the future.

Faith-Praying

God told Abraham, the man of faith, "Lift your eyes now and look from the place where you are—northward, southward, eastward, and westward; for all the land which you see I give to you and your descendants forever" (Gen. 13:14–15 NKJV). Similarly, God placed a vision in Jerry Falwell's heart that the mountain of his youth would one day become instrumental in God's plan for His ministry.

That was a faith-vision.

In Joshua 1:3, God told Joshua, "I have given you every place where the sole of your foot treads, just as I promised Moses." In that same sense, Jerry Falwell prayed for the finances to purchase the mountain, then prayed for money to build the buildings, and then, by faith, prayed for students to be trained on the mountain.

This is faith-praying.

Jerry was once asked, "How did you get such big faith?"

He responded very candidly, saying, "I don't have great faith in God; I have faith in a great God."

When you ask God for faith, He doesn't zap you and give you the ability to move mountains, or even get rid of pebbles in your shoes. Rather, when you ask for faith to move mountains, He gives you mountains to climb (a vision to accomplish great things) and helps you climb those mountains. Jerry said on many occasions, "Your faith is not something you measure. You measure God, the One in whom you trust."

A Burgeoning Faith

Jerry was also once asked, "How did you get a view of such a big God?"

He said that his view of God was developed while he was a student at Baptist Bible College, in Springfield, Missouri, during his first year. While attending High Street Baptist Church in Springfield—one of the early megachurches, with more than 2,000 people in attendance—Pastor W. E. Dowell suggested that Jerry teach a Sunday school class in the junior department.

Max Hawkins, the junior Sunday school superintendent at that time, wasn't sure that he wanted to give Jerry one of his better classes. So he had an associate string up two curtains in the corner of an assembly area and gave Jerry a roll book and one fourth-grade student. Jerry taught that boy, Daryl, for three weeks and then went to Max Hawkins, saying, "You haven't gotten me any other students to teach, so I think I'll quit."

Max said to him, "That's exactly what I figured."

The superintendent went on to tell Jerry he didn't want to give him a class because he felt Jerry was just a puffy-cheeked young freshman who would give up when the first opposition came. He reached for the roll book that Jerry was holding.

"No," Jerry abruptly said, jerking back the book. "I'll take the class and I'll make it a success."

Jerry subsequently got a key to an empty dormitory room and, as soon as lunch was over, he began going to that room every day to pray and read the great classic books of the Christian life until dinnertime. He read the biography of George Mueller (a man he considered to have the greatest faith since the apostle Paul), *Absolute Surrender* by Andrew Murray (his favorite author), *Power Through Prayer* by E. M. Bounds, *Normal Christian Life* by Watchman Nee and *The Christian's Secret of a Happy Life* by Hannah Whitall Smith, and many books that encouraged his faith. He also began to learn that prayer was a relationship with God, as we see in Hebrews 11:6: "For the one who draws near to Him must believe that He exists and rewards those who seek Him."

It was in that dormitory room that Jerry learned to know God and to trust God. And his life was forever changed.

Bold-Faith Believing

In the early 1970s on an occasion when Jerry was flying into Lynchburg, he looked down on Liberty Mountain, knowing that it was the spot where Liberty University would one day stand. He asked a real estate agent who was sitting beside him, "Who owns that property?"

The agent replied, "U.S. Gypsum."

Jerry asked, "Is it for sale?"

The agent responded, "*Everything* is for sale."

It was then that Jerry again walked that mountain, claiming every square foot of the four thousand acres for God.

Later Jerry phoned U.S. Gypsum headquarters and made an appointment to talk with the vice president in charge of real estate. With the same real estate agent with him, Jerry flew to Chicago to negotiate buying the land.

"How did you know the land was for sale?" the vice president asked Jerry.

At a recent board meeting, U.S. Gypsum had decided to sell off real estate holdings across America and they wanted $1,250,000 for the mountain in Lynchburg. The property had not been advertised, nor had anyone been told outside their organization that it was for sale.

Jerry knew the power of vision, so he shared the heaven-inspired vision of building a great Christian university on the mountain. He then he asked if he could give a down payment on the property. At that moment Jerry had no idea where the money was coming from, except he knew it would come from God. He knew that God wanted them to have the land and that God would consequently supply the money.

The vice president said he'd take a $100,000 down payment.

Jerry said that he had a check with him for $10,000 and asked if that would be enough for him to hold the land until he could get the $100,000.

"Yes," the vice president laughed, not quite sure what to make of this small-town pastor with the audacious faith. Jerry left that day assuring the vice president that he could raise the $90,000 during the next two months.

As Jerry was leaving the office he added, "Don't cash that $10,000 check for three or four days; I've got to raise enough money to cover that!"

The vice president really began to laugh at that point.

We worship a God of miracles and He was not about to put a vision in the heart of Jerry Falwell and then leave him in the lurch. Within two months of that meeting, Jerry had raised the necessary $100,000 as down payment on the future Liberty Mountain.

It is bold-faith believing that leads to bold-faith vision and results in bold-faith praying.

Bold Vision

Let's go back to the beginning. Jerry Falwell began Thomas Road Baptist Church on June 25, 1957, in Mountain View Elementary School, where he had attended first grade. The following week he drove in a pickup truck belonging to one of his members, Pop Johnson, around Lynchburg, looking for a permanent home for the infant church. The only place suitable was a bankrupt and abandoned Donald Duck Bottling Plant, where Donald Duck Cola had been made. The building was full of a syrupy film and the yard was overgrown with weeds. Plywood covered the windows and the doors were padlocked. It hardly resembled a church.

While Jerry and Pop were examining the facility, a thunderstorm rolled in from the west and they hurried back to the pickup. Through the rain-soaked windshield, Jerry and Pop Johnson looked at the improbable site.

"It's not what I expected," Jerry said.

"It's all we've got," Pop replied. "Let's use it till something better comes along."

Jerry responded, "We can make this place famous for the gospel, Pop. What goes on inside will be more important than the building."

Then, looking down the long stretch of Thomas Road, where the bottling plant resided. He began to dream of expansion down the hill. He imagined a massive sanctuary with plenty of classrooms and an accommodating parking lot.

With that vision in his mind, he told Pop, "We'll reach all of Lynchburg. Then from this place, we can touch the world."

As the rain pounded on the roof of the truck, Jerry began to pray. The world might have seen two men praying in a truck on that day, but God looked down and saw the faith of two intercessors, and He determined to answer their prayers.

Thomas Road Baptist Church was Falwell's bold vision and bold faith, and everything that's been accomplished has been an answer to bold prayer.

Bold-Faith Initiative

People might say that first Sunday in the building was anything but glorious. Even though the women had scrubbed the floor with Clorox, people's shoes stuck to the floor. It would be weeks before they fully got rid of the sticky substance that clung to their shoes. Members had also washed the inside of the windows but hadn't had time to clean the outside. Sunlight poured in through the heavy dust. But to Jerry Falwell and Pop Johnson and the members of the new church, the building was indeed glorious! It was their platform to carry the gospel to their community and ultimately throughout the world.

By faith, Jerry knew that if he shared the gospel with enough people, many would get saved and come to the new Thomas Road Baptist Church. He committed himself to making one hundred visits to homes in the local area every day, except Sunday. He began early every morning, knocking on doors. He frequently visited well into the evening, sometimes until nine o'clock. Next, the ladies began mailing a church newsletter to all of the potential members that Jerry met in his visitations. There was a corporate effort to evangelize Lynchburg.

Within a few weeks Jerry had covered every home within a one-mile radius of the church. And so he began on the second phase of his visitation plan, which included homes within a two-mile radius of the new church. In his deep faith Jerry believed that when he went door to door, according to the Scriptural pattern, God would bless and send people to his church.

On the first anniversary of Thomas Road Baptist Church, God had indeed blessed. The church welcomed 857 people for that service. A year later, on its second anniversary, the church had doubled that number.

The church was growing as a result of Jerry Falwell's bold-faith initiative.

Bold Faith and Bold Plans

In the fall of 1956, three months after beginning the church, Jerry decided to begin his own daily radio broadcast. He talked to a Mr. Epperson, owner of Lynchburg's WBRG 105.00 AM, about initiating a broadcast.

Mr. Epperson told Jerry, "Don't just have a weekly broadcast; go on the radio every day, Reverend." Mr. Epperson had actually been looking for someone to start his broadcast day with a faith-related broadcast.

"You'd be just perfect," he told Jerry.

And with his typical bold exuberance, Jerry began an early-morning daily radio broadcast. It cost the new church $7 a day. WBRG was a Country & Western station, which captured the hearts of the blue collar workers of Lynchburg. Jerry knew that they were the kind of people that comprised Thomas Road Baptist Church, so it was a perfect fit.

Each morning Jerry began with a theme song, "We've Come This Far by Faith." He would then share with his audience what God was doing at the new church. He told story after story of people getting saved and lives being changed there. Many of the listeners recognized the name of the converts and came to see what God was doing at the church in the old bottling plant. The broadcast allowed him to stir up even more excitement about the growing new church. And as people began to respond to the radio broadcast, Jerry headed out to visit them.

A month into the new radio broadcast, the always-advancing Jerry decided the church needed to go on television. This was a seemingly preposterous plan, especially when you consider that none of the well-established churches in the area were on television at the time. In fact, very few churches in America had a television broadcast at that time.

Bold-Faith Praying

Bold faith and bold praying brought Jerry's God-inspired plans into reality. He was able to secure a half-hour slot every Sunday from 5:30 to 6:00 p.m. The small ABC outlet on Lynchburg's Main Street had a two-man crew to work the two cameras for the live broadcast.

The audience heard, "Hello, my name is Jerry Falwell, and I am the pastor of Thomas Road Baptist Church."

On the broadcast Jerry began telling people about how God called him to return to his hometown to start a church, how the church was growing, and how lives were being dramatically changed.

In addition to the new radio and TV broadcasts, Thomas Road Baptist Church had begun construction on a new building—just four months after beginning services in the old bottling plant. The church was the big news in Lynchburg.

Jerry was excited about the new construction. During his television broadcast, Jerry would sometimes say: "You've got plenty of time to eat a peanut butter sandwich, drink a glass of milk, grab your Bible, and come on over to Thomas Road Baptist Church, where I will welcome you personally." Thirty minutes later, the Sunday evening service began, with Jerry preaching.

The story of God's blessing on Jerry Falwell and Thomas Road Baptist Church is a picture of bold vision and bold faith, with each leading to bold praying.

There was an empty compressor room in back of the Donald Duck plant that originally held the carbonation tanks. A group of laymen began gathering in that room while Jerry was preaching on live television to pray for their young pastor. The room had a red mud floor, so the men dragged in a piece of carpet and placed it on a 4x8 piece of plywood. There these intercessors, common men of prayer, began banging on the windows of heaven, asking God to help their little church capture the city of Lynchburg and ultimately touch the world.

When God heard these dedicated men in bold-faith praying, I imagine that God turned to His angels and said, "Let's give them the things they are asking so that millions of people can be reached for Christ."

Bold Prayer

In the fall of 1978, construction on seven three-story dormitories was initiated on Liberty Mountain, near the little Prayer Chapel that serves to remind all visitors to Liberty of the importance of the local church. During the construction on these dorms, the school ran out of money. And for six months those buildings sat as empty shells. However, they also served a purpose by calling Christians to the challenge of prayer.

The following spring Jerry stood at the podium during a Liberty chapel service, saying, "We're scrapping our program for chapel today. Instead, we're going to go pray for the funds to complete the seven dormitory buildings up on the hill." He then instructed the Liberty students, faculty, and staff who had faith in God to supply the need for the urgently needed dorms to follow him.

Everyone attending that chapel service followed Jerry out of the building, not quite sure where he was leading them. He walked straight up the hill to the site of the unfinished dorms and said that the gathering was going to walk around each dorm one time.

Jerry boldly stated, "Joshua walked around Jericho seven times, but we don't have the time to do that during the chapel hour today. So we'll walk around just once. After that, we will break up into groups of seven, kneel down, and pray for the money to finish constructing the dorms."

On my knees with six others, I prayed that day, "Lord, five million dollars is more than I've ever thought of. I've never prayed for that much money before. I don't have faith to trust You for five million dollars. 'Lord, I believe; help Thou my unbelief.'"

As my group prayed, I heard Jerry praying. He said, "Lord, You've got a lot of money and I need some of it to finish these dormitories." Then he reminded God, "When these dormitories are finished, eight hundred more students can come to Liberty. They will be missionaries, businessmen, teachers, and pastors."

Jerry didn't beg for money, nor did he repeatedly ask for it. In great confidence of faith, he simply said, "Lord, I believe You're going to supply this money to train these students, so tomorrow I'm telling the contractors to begin their work. I'll need money for the first 'draw' to pay the contractors two weeks from now."

I later wrote about this story in one of my books. For this project, I interviewed Macel Falwell, Jerry's wife. I asked her, "Did Jerry really believe the money was coming in?"

"Absolutely!" she exclaimed.

"Was there any crack in his faith when he asked for five million dollars?" I asked her.

"None whatsoever," she said with a smile. She had seen Jerry continually launch out by faith, fully confident that God would not abandon him.

Bold vision and bold faith leads to bold prayers.

Confidence of Faith

I want to close by recounting an episode from the life of Jerry Falwell that defines his daring faith and distinctive dependence on prayer.

It was an average spring morning at Liberty University. On this day, as the vice presidents and other campus leaders arrived in a little room behind the stage where our chapels take place, we learned that Vernon Brewer, Liberty's then-vice president of student relations, had been diagnosed with stomach cancer. We were further shocked to learn that Vernon had been told by doctors that he had been given no more than six months to live.

When Jerry walked in the room and heard the news, he responded in a way that can only be defined as "typical Falwell." Jerry said, "We can't let Vernon die; he's important to the work of Liberty. We've got to change God's mind, so let's fast and pray."

Jerry walked to the chapel platform that day and announced to our then-five thousand students, our faculty and staff that Vernon had been given only a short time to live. He then said, "We are going to fast and pray—all of us—and we will beseech God to turn this situation around."

Jerry announced that the school cafeteria would be closed for the next twenty-four hours. There would be no meal that evening, no breakfast the next morning, nor any lunch the next day. This type of fast is known as a *Yom Kippur* fast. All of the Liberty students agreed to fast for Vernon's healing. (The cafeteria did accommodate those students with health problems who could not fast.)

Jerry then told those gathered in that special chapel meeting, "I don't want you to just pray as you walk around the campus or pray a little bit here or a little bit there; rather I want you to go to the prayer chapel and spend one hour on your knees before God, asking for a miracle."

He then shared with students an important lesson on prayer from Jesus, by referencing Matthew 26:40: "Could you not watch with Me one hour?" (NKJV). Jerry urged every student, faculty member and staffer to commit to at least one hour of prayer so that we would be jointly calling out to God to heal Vernon Brewer.

That morning as Jerry was calling for this intense prayer drive, I was standing next to Vernon Brewer on the platform. I sensed God's voice telling me: "Place your hands on Vernon's head to pray." I didn't want to look like a fanatic in front of all the students, so in my heart I said no. I suddenly realized, however, that I was saying no to the Lord. Then I said to myself, "You can't call Him Lord and then tell Him no."

Immediately I confessed my unbelief and laid my hands on Vernon's head and began earnestly praying for his healing. As I prayed, I had a sudden assurance in my heart that God was going to heal my friend.

This is called the "prayer of faith [that] will save the sick" (James 5:15). The prayer of faith is described as a prayer you offer, knowing you will get the answer even before it comes. I do not claim that it was my prayers that healed Vernon; rather, it was the prayers of five thousand students and others as they joined their hearts together to beseech God to act on behalf of Vernon Brewer that brought about his healing.

God heard our prayers and touched Vernon with an extraordinary healing.

Through my years of friendship with Jerry Falwell, I heard him say on several occasions, "There is value in the volume of prayer."

There was certainly power in the prayer for Vernon. God honored our prayers. God wanted Vernon healed.

Today Vernon Brewer heads World Help, an organization that provides more than $25 million worldwide in evangelism and humanitarian aid. He is honoring the God that healed him.

Every April 25, I phone Vernon to remind him of that wondrous day. I typically say to him, "Ain't God good?" We laugh and rejoice in God's healing and intervention.

Vernon always replies, "I just had my health checkup and there's no sign of cancer."

It's now been twenty-four years since doctors told him he had only a short time to live!

Jerry had a bold vision to see his friend healed. He also had bold faith, fully believing that if everyone joined their hearts in prayer, they could touch the heart of God. Through Jerry's bold praying, we saw one of many great miracles that have defined the existence of Liberty University through the course of its brief history.

I miss my dear friend Jerry Falwell. He was such an encourager and daring representative of Jesus Christ. It is my honor to tell about this amazing man and allow his life of faith to continue to inspire and encourage others to audaciously live out their faith in our Lord Jesus Christ.

Some churches have narrowed their vision. They are focusing only on maintaining their flock. As a result, they are not influencing many areas of their communities with the gospel. We cannot lead our churches under a mantle of fear or trepidation about how our message may be received. We must look to the apostle Paul as our mentor in boldly taking the gospel to all areas of society.

Our goals of innovation should come through methods of invigorating our worship experience or finding new means to plant churches or discovering new manners in which we can confront the culture through "salt and light" ministry. My passion is to use the innovational methods described in this book to help pastors and church leaders around the nation to consider new means of taking the gospel to their own communities.

During my journey of discovery regarding the fifty-one years of innovative ministry at Thomas Road Baptist Church, I found that the church has always been active within eight major areas of ministry. I believe these eight areas, as defined in this book, should be the backbone of every church's desire to become more proactive in outreach and Christian influence.

In my opinion, churches can reach their greatest potential and purpose by fully engaging in all of these areas. We cannot afford to cherry pick the areas of greater interest. Further, we must be involved and passionate about all of them, especially those that require us to step outside our comfort zones. I think many churches need to relearn the basics so that they can reinvigorate their efforts to impact their communities with the gospel.

In this book, we have attempted to make the case for all eight of these areas. It is my deep desire to cast the vision to pastors and lay people everywhere to get involved in all of them to fully experience your church's potential for Christ. I trust that you will study this book, meditate on its points, thoughtfully process its premise, and ultimately begin to implement its designs and methods.

While the title of this book talks about innovation in the church, the real innovation comes from taking our churches back to the future. Found within our roots are foundational truths that will guide our churches to greater heights in the days to come. While I am fully supportive and engaged in using brand new methods to reach the lost in our nation and world, I am also fully aware that those methods can never trump what is not new—the basics that have worked for ages. Innovating (or altering) the foundational message of the gospel is simply not an option.

Contributors

Jonathan Falwell is the senior pastor of Thomas Road Baptist Church in Lynchburg, Virginia. He served at TRBC under the leadership of his father and founding pastor, Dr. Jerry Falwell, from 1995 until his father's death in May 2007. Jonathan earned his Bachelor of Science degree from Liberty University, his Master of Arts in Religion from the Liberty Baptist Theological Seminary, and his law degree (Juris Doctor) from William Howard Taft University.

Doug Randlett is the executive pastor of Thomas Road Baptist Church in Lynchburg, Virginia. Doug recently returned to Lynchburg following nine years of ministry with Christ Fellowship, Palm Beach Gardens, Florida, where he was the campus pastor at the regional site in Royal Palm Beach. Prior to that he served more than twenty years at Liberty University as Chairman of the Church Ministries Department and as an associate pastor at Thomas Road Baptist Church.

Matt Willmington is an associate pastor at Thomas Road Baptist Church. He served at Liberty University for thirteen years as a youth ministry trainer and an associate professor in the School of Religion. He ministered as executive pastor and small groups pastor at West Ridge Church in Dallas, Georgia, for eight years. Matt did his undergraduate and seminary work at Liberty and has an Ed.D. from Argosy University at Sarasota.

Charles Billingsley serves as worship leader at Thomas Road Baptist Church in Lynchburg, Virginia. He also serves as Artist-in-Residence for the 10,000 resident students at Liberty University and is a senior advisor to more than 500 students of the Liberty University Center for Worship. In addition to his schedule at the church, Charles leads worship and performs solo concerts about a hundred times a year.

Rod Dempsey is the discipleship pastor at Thomas Road Baptist Church and the chairman of Discipleship Ministries at Liberty Baptist Theological Seminary. He is the coauthor of *The Pocket Guide to Leading a Small Group* and writes frequently for *SmallGroups.com* magazine. Prior to coming to Thomas Road, he served as a church planter, Christian education pastor, membership/assimilation pastor, small group pastor, and elder.

David Wheeler is a professor of evangelism and associate director of the Church Planting and Ministry Training Center for Liberty Baptist Theological Seminary. Dr. Wheeler is widely known for his publications related to servant evangelism and strategic evangelism planning for the local church. He is also an accomplished conference leader and motivational speaker.

Dave Earley is an experienced church planter and coach. He serves as the director of the Liberty Center for Church Planting at Liberty University. He is also chairman of the Department of Pastoral Leadership and Church Planning for Liberty Baptist Theological Seminary. He has authored eleven books on subjects such as small groups, leadership, prayer, and the Christian life.

Ergun Caner is president of Liberty Baptist Theological Seminary. Dr. Caner became the first former Muslim to become the leader of an evangelical seminary. Along with his brother Emir, Caner has become a leading voice for evangelicalism on the national stage. He has been a guest on such networks as FOX News, MSNBC, CNBC, the BBC, and TBN.

Ed Hindson is assistant chancellor and professor of Old Testament Studies and Eschatology at Liberty University in Lynchburg, Virginia. The veteran educator and theologian has authored twenty books. He edited the Gold Medallion Award-winning *Knowing Jesus Study Bible* and coedited the Tim LaHaye *Prophecy Study Bible*. Dr. Hindson also hosts *The King Is Coming*, a syndicated television broadcast dealing with Bible prophecy.

J. M. Smith is the former editor of *The National Liberty Journal*. He also coproduced, with Dr. Jerry Falwell, the Listen America radio broadcast. He has written for several national publications and continues to produce, with Jonathan Falwell, *The Falwell Confidential*, a weekly news e-mail that was initiated by Dr. Jerry Falwell in 1996. Pastors and church leaders interested in a free subscription to the e-mail, which is received by more than 250,000 people worldwide, may sign up at www.falwell.com.

Mathew D. Staver, founder and chairman of Liberty Counsel, has argued in numerous state and federal courts across the country, including the United States Supreme Court. He also serves as dean of Liberty University School of Law and is a trustee for the Supreme Court Historical Society. Mat is considered one of the premier constitutional litigators in the country and conducts hundreds of media interviews each year, including television appearances on shows such as *The O'Reilly Factor, Hannity and Colmes, Anderson Cooper 360, Good Morning America, The Today Show, Fox & Friends*, and many other broadcasts.

Daniel Henderson has joined the staff of Thomas Road Baptist Church after serving as senior pastor of several very large churches. He is the pastor of renewal and teaches part-time at Liberty University. Strategic Renewal exists to ignite the heart of the church through personal renewal, congregational revival, and leadership restoration.

Elmer Towns, cofounder of Liberty University, is a college and seminary professor, an author of popular and scholarly works (the editor of two encyclopedias), a popular seminar lecturer, and dedicated worker in Sunday school. He has developed more than twenty resource packets for leadership education. Dr. Towns, a prolific writer, has authored one hundred twenty-five books.